Just The

facts101
Textbook Key Facts

Textbook Outlines, Highlights, and Practice Quizzes

Drugs, Society and Human Behavior

by Carl Hart, 15th Edition

All "Just the Facts101" Material Written or Prepared by Cram101 Publishing

Title Page

"Just the Facts101" is a Cram101 publication and tool designed to give you all the facts from your textbooks. Visit Cram101.com for the full practice test for each of your chapters for virtually any of your textbooks.

Cram101 has built custom study tools specific to your textbook. We provide all of the factual testable information and unlike traditional study guides, we will never send you back to your textbook for more information.

YOU WILL NEVER HAVE TO HIGHLIGHT A BOOK AGAIN!

Cram101 StudyGuides
All of the information in this StudyGuide is written specifically for your textbook. We include the key terms, places, people, and concepts... the information you can expect on your next exam!

Want to take a practice test?
Throughout each chapter of this StudyGuide you will find links to cram101.com where you can select specific chapters to take a complete test on, or you can subscribe and get practice tests for up to 12 of your textbooks, along with other exclusive cram101.com tools like problem solving labs and reference libraries.

Cram101.com
Only cram101.com gives you the outlines, highlights, and PRACTICE TESTS specific to your textbook. Cram101.com is an online application where you'll discover study tools designed to make the most of your limited study time.

By purchasing this book, you get 50% off the normal monthly subscription fee!. Just enter the promotional code **'DK73DW22005'** on the Cram101.com registration screen.

www.Cram101.com

Drugs, Society and Human Behavior
Carl Hart, 15th

CONTENTS

CHAPTER OUTLINE: KEY TERMS, PEOPLE, PLACES, CONCEPTS

	Administration
	Methamphetamine
	Cocaine
	Dose-response relationship
	Prescription
	Adderall
	Substance-related disorder
	Amphetamine
	War on Drugs
	Monitoring
	Psychoactive drug
	Self-help group
	Protective factor
	Risk factor
	Social influence
	Screening
	Antecedent
	Controlled substance
	Impulsivity
	Substance abuse
	Longitudinal study

1. Drug Use: An Overview

_____ | Social skill
_____ | Variable
_____ | Confession
_____ | Ronald Reagan
_____ | Consciousness
_____ | Drug user
_____ | Reinforcement

Administration	As a legal concept, administration is a procedure under the insolvency laws of a number of common law jurisdictions. It functions as a rescue mechanism for insolvent entities and allows them to carry on running their business. The process - an alternative to liquidation - is often known as going into administration.
Methamphetamine	Methamphetamine is a psychostimulant of the phenethylamine and amphetamine class of drugs. It increases alertness, concentration, energy, and in high doses, can induce euphoria, enhances self-esteem, and increase libido. Methamphetamine has high potential for abuse and addiction by activating the psychological reward system via triggering a cascading release of dopamine and norepinephrine in the brain.
Cocaine	Cocaine is a 1922 British crime film directed by Graham Cutts and starring Hilda Bayley, Flora Le Breton, Ward McAllister and Cyril Raymond. A melodrama - it depicts the distribution of cocaine by gangsters through a series of London nightclubs and the revenge sought by a man after the death of his daughter.
	Because of its depiction of drug use, it was the most controversial British film of the 1920s.
Dose-response relationship	The dose-response relationship, describes the change in effect on an organism caused by differing levels of exposure (or doses) to a stressor (usually a chemical) after a certain exposure time .

This may apply to individuals (e.g.: a small amount has no significant effect, a large amount is fatal), or to populations (e.g.: how many people or organisms are affected at different levels of exposure).

Studying dose response, and developing dose response models, is central to determining 'safe' and 'hazardous' levels and dosages for drugs, potential pollutants, and other substances to which humans or other organisms are exposed.

Prescription	In law, prescription is the method of sovereignty transfer of a territory through international law analogous to the common law doctrine of adverse possession for private real-estate. Prescription involves the open encroachment by the new sovereign upon the territory in question for a prolonged period of time, acting as the sovereign, without protest or other contest by the original sovereign. This doctrine legalizes de jure the de facto transfer of sovereignty caused in part by the original sovereign's extended negligence and/or neglect of the area in question.
Adderall	Adderall is a brand-name psychostimulant medication composed of racemic amphetamine aspartate monohydrate, racemic amphetamine sulfate, dextroamphetamine saccharide, and dextroamphetamine sulfate, which is thought by scientists to work by increasing the amount of dopamine and norepinephrine in the brain. In addition, the drug also acts as a potent dopamine reuptake inhibitor and norepinephrine reuptake inhibitor. Adderall is widely reported to increase alertness, increase libido, increase concentration and overall cognitive performance, and, in general, improve mood, while decreasing user fatigue.
Substance-related disorder	A substance-related disorder is an umbrella term used to describe several different conditions (such as intoxication, harmful use/abuse, dependence, withdrawal, and psychoses or amnesia associated with the use of the substance) associated with several different substances (such as alcohol or opiods).
Amphetamine	Amphetamine or amfetamine (INN) is a psychostimulant drug of the phenethylamine class which produces increased wakefulness and focus in association with decreased fatigue and appetite. Brand names of medications that contain, or metabolize into, amphetamine include Adderall, Dexedrine, Dextrostat, Desoxyn, ProCentra, and Vyvanse, as well as Benzedrine in the past. The drug is also used recreationally and as a performance enhancer.
War on Drugs	The War on Drugs is a controversial campaign of prohibition and foreign military aid and military intervention being undertaken by the United States government, with the assistance of participating countries, intended to both define and reduce the illegal drug trade. This initiative includes a set of drug policies of the United States that are intended to discourage the production, distribution, and consumption of illegal psychoactive drugs.

1. Drug Use: An Overview

Monitoring	In medicine, monitoring is the evaluation of a disease or condition over time. It can be performed by continuously measuring certain parameters (for example, by continuously measuring vital signs by a bedside monitor), and/or by repeatedly performing medical tests (such as blood glucose monitoring in people with diabetes mellitus). Transmitting data from a monitor to a distant monitoring station is known as telemetry or biotelemetry.
Psychoactive drug	A psychoactive drug, psychopharmaceutical, or psychotropic is a chemical substance that crosses the blood-brain barrier and acts primarily upon the central nervous system where it affects brain function, resulting in changes in perception, mood, consciousness, cognition, and behavior. These substances may be used recreationally, to purposefully alter one's consciousness, as entheogens, for ritual, spiritual, and/or shamanic purposes, as a tool for studying or augmenting the mind, or therapeutically as medication. Because psychoactive substances bring about subjective changes in consciousness and mood that the user may find pleasant (e.g. euphoria) or advantageous (e.g. increased alertness), many psychoactive substances are abused, that is, used excessively, despite health risks or negative consequences.
Self-help group	A self-help group (SHG) is a village-based financial intermediary usually composed of 10-20 local women. Most self-help groups are located in India, though SHGs can also be found in other countries, especially in South Asia and Southeast Asia. Members make small regular savings contributions over a few months until there is enough capital in the group to begin lending.
Protective factor	Protective factors are conditions or attributes (skills, strengths, resources, supports or coping strategies) in individuals, families, communities or the larger society that help people deal more effectively with stressful events and mitigate or eliminate risk in families and communities. Protective factors include:•Adoptive parents having an accurate understanding of their adopted children's pre-adoption medical and behavioral problems •Assistance of adoption professionals in the home of adopted children Some risks that adopted children are prone to :•Self-mutilation•Delinquency•Trouble with the law•Substance abuse•Thievery.
Risk factor	Risk factor research has proliferated within the discipline of Criminology in recent years, based largely on the early work of Sheldon and Eleanor Glueck in the USA and David Farrington in the UK.

The identification of risk factors that are allegedly predictive of offending and reoffending (especially by young people) has heavily influenced the criminal justice policies and practices of a number of first world countries, notably the UK, the USA and Australia. However, the robustness and validity of much 'artefactual' risk factor research has recently come under sustained criticism for:

- Reductionism - e.g. over-simplifying complex experiences and circumstances by converting them to simple quantities, limiting investigation of risk factors to psychological and immediate social domains of life, whilst neglecting socio-structural influences;

- Determinism - e.g. characterising young people as passive victims of risk experiences with no ability to construct, negotiate or resist risk;

- Imputation - e.g. assuming that risk factors and definitions of offending are homogenous across countries and cultures, assuming that statistical correlations between risk factors and offending actually represent causal relationships, assuming that risk factors apply to individuals on the basis of aggregated data.

Two UK academics, Stephen Case and Kevin Haines, have been particularly forceful in their critique of risk factor research within a number of academic papers and a comprehensive polemic text entitled 'Understanding Youth Offending: Risk Factor Research, Policy and Practice'.

Social influence	Social influence occurs when one's emotions, opinions, or behaviors are affected by others. Social influence takes many forms and can be seen in conformity, socialization, peer pressure, obedience, leadership, persuasion, sales, and marketing. In 1958, Harvard psychologist, Herbert Kelman identified three broad varieties of social influence.
Screening	Screening in economics refers to a strategy of combating adverse selection, one of the potential decision-making complications in cases of asymmetric information. The concept of screening was first developed by Michael Spence (1973), and should be distinguished from signalling, which implies that the informed agent moves first. For purposes of screening, asymmetric information cases assume two economic agents--which we call, for example, Abel and Cain--where Abel knows more about himself than Cain knows about Abel.
Antecedent	In genealogy or in phylogenetic studies of evolutionary biology an antecedent, antecessor or antecedents are predecessors in a family line. I am the descendants of my grandparents, they are my antecedents. This term has particular utility in evolutionary coalescent theory, which models the process of genetic drift in reverse time.

1. Drug Use: An Overview

Controlled substance	A controlled substance is generally a drug or chemical whose manufacture, possession, and use are regulated by a government. This may include illegal drugs and prescription medications (designated Controlled Drug in the United Kingdom).
Impulsivity	Impulsivity is a personality trait characterized by the inclination of an individual to initiate behavior without adequate forethought as to the consequences of their actions, acting on the spur of the moment. Eysenck and Eysenck related impulsivity to risk-taking, lack of planning, and making up one's mind quickly. Impulsivity has been shown to be a major component of various neuropsychiatric disorders such as ADHD, substance abuse disorders and bipolar disorder.
Substance abuse	Substance abuse, also known as drug abuse, is a patterned use of a substance (drug) in which the user consumes the substance in amounts or with methods neither approved nor supervised by medical professionals. Substance abuse/drug abuse is not limited to mood-altering or psycho-active drugs. If an activity is performed using the objects against the rules and policies of the matter (as in steroids for performance enhancement in sports), it is also called substance abuse.
Longitudinal study	A longitudinal study is a correlational research study that involves repeated observations of the same variables over long periods of time -- often many decades. It is a type of observational study. Longitudinal studies are often used in psychology to study developmental trends across the life span, and in sociology to study life events throughout lifetimes or generations.
Social skill	A social skill is any skill facilitating interaction and communication with others. Social rules and relations are created, communicated, and changed in verbal and nonverbal ways. The process of learning such skills is called socialization.
Variable	In mathematics, a variable is a value that may change within the scope of a given problem or set of operations. In contrast, a constant is a value that remains unchanged, though often unknown or undetermined. The concepts of constants and variables are fundamental to many areas of mathematics and its applications.
Confession	In the law of criminal evidence, a confession is a statement by a suspect in crime which is adverse to that person. Some authorities, such as Black's Law Dictionary, define a confession in more narrow terms, e.g. as 'a statement admitting or acknowledging all facts necessary for conviction of a crime,' which would be distinct from a mere admission of certain facts that, if true, would still not, by themselves, satisfy all the elements of the offense. This specific form of testimony, involving oneself, is used as a form of proof in judicial matters, since at least the Inquisition.
Ronald Reagan	Ronald Wilson Reagan (; February 6, 1911 - June 5, 2004) was the 40th President of the United States, serving from 1981 to 1989. Prior to that, he was the 33rd Governor of California from 1967 to 1975 and a radio, film and television actor.

Born in Tampico, Illinois and raised in Dixon, Reagan was educated at Eureka College, earning a Bachelor of Arts degree in economics and sociology. After his graduation, Reagan moved first to Iowa to work as a radio broadcaster and then in to Los Angeles, California in 1937 where he began a career as an actor, first in films and later television. Some of his most notable films include Knute Rockne, All American, Kings Row, and Bedtime for Bonzo. Reagan served as president of the Screen Actors Guild, and later as a spokesman for General Electric (GE); his start in politics occurred during his work for GE. Originally a member of the Democratic Party, his positions began shifting rightward in the late 1950s, and he switched to the Republican Party in 1962. After delivering a rousing speech in support of Barry Goldwater's presidential candidacy in 1964, he was persuaded to seek the California governorship, winning two years later and again in 1970. He was defeated in his run for the Republican presidential nomination in 1968 as well as 1976, but won both the nomination and election in 1980, defeating incumbent Jimmy Carter.

As president, Reagan implemented sweeping new political and economic initiatives. His supply-side economic policies, dubbed 'Reaganomics', advocated reducing tax rates to spur economic growth, controlling the money supply to reduce inflation, deregulation of the economy, and reducing government spending. In his first term he survived an assassination attempt, took a hard line against labor unions, and ordered an invasion of Grenada. He was reelected in a landslide in 1984, proclaiming that it was 'Morning in America.' His second term was primarily marked by foreign matters, such as the ending of the Cold War, the 1986 bombing of Libya, and the revelation of the Iran-Contra affair. Publicly describing the Soviet Union as an 'evil empire,' he supported anti-communist movements worldwide and spent his first term forgoing the strategy of détente by ordering a massive military buildup in an arms race with the USSR. Reagan negotiated with Soviet General Secretary Mikhail Gorbachev, culminating in the INF Treaty and the decrease of both countries' nuclear arsenals.

Reagan left office in 1989. In 1994, the former president disclosed that he had been diagnosed with Alzheimer's disease earlier in the year; he died ten years later at the age of 93. He ranks highly in public opinion polls of U.S. Presidents and is credited for generating an ideological renaissance on the American political right. Early life

Ronald Wilson Reagan was born in an apartment on the second floor of a commercial building in Tampico, Illinois on February 6, 1911, to Jack Reagan and Nelle Wilson Reagan. Reagan's father was a salesman and a storyteller, the grandson of Irish Catholic immigrants from County Tipperary while his mother had Scots and English ancestors. Reagan had one sibling, his older brother, Neil (1908-1996), who became an advertising executive. As a boy, Reagan's father nicknamed his son 'Dutch', due to his 'fat little Dutchman'-like appearance, and his 'Dutchboy' haircut; the nickname stuck with him throughout his youth. Reagan's family briefly lived in several towns and cities in Illinois, including Monmouth, Galesburg and Chicago, until 1919, when they returned to Tampico and lived above the H.C. Pitney Variety Store.

1. Drug Use: An Overview

After his election as president, residing in the upstairs White House private quarters, Reagan would quip that he was 'living above the store again'.

According to Paul Kengor, author of God and Ronald Reagan, Reagan had a particularly strong faith in the goodness of people, which stemmed from the optimistic faith of his mother, Nelle, and the Disciples of Christ faith, which he was baptized into in 1922. For the time, Reagan was unusual in his opposition to racial discrimination, and recalled a time in Dixon when the local inn would not allow black people to stay there.

Consciousness	Consciousness is the quality or state of being aware of an external object or something within oneself. It has been defined as: subjectivity, awareness, sentience, the ability to experience or to feel, wakefulness, having a sense of selfhood, and the executive control system of the mind. Despite the difficulty in definition, many philosophers believe that there is a broadly shared underlying intuition about what consciousness is.
Drug user	A drug user is a person who uses drugs either legally or illegally. The term user is typically employed more to refer to illegal drug use by a person who is often part of a subculture of recreational drug use. Drug users are often referred to as 'heads', depending on the drug used, i.e., pothead, hophead, crackhead, etc.
Reinforcement	Reinforcement is a term in operant conditioning and behavior analysis for a process of strengthening a directly measurable dimension of behavior-such as rate (e.g., pulling a lever more frequently), duration (e.g., pulling a lever for longer periods of time), magnitude (e.g., pulling a lever with greater force), or latency (e.g., pulling a lever more quickly following the onset of an environmental event)-as a function of the delivery of a stimulus (e.g. money from a slot machine) immediately or shortly after the occurrence of the behavior. Giving a monkey a banana for performing a trick is an example of positive reinforcement.

Reinforcement is only said to have occurred if the delivery of the stimulus is directly caused by the response made. |

1. _____ is the quality or state of being aware of an external object or something within oneself. It has been defined as: subjectivity, awareness, sentience, the ability to experience or to feel, wakefulness, having a sense of selfhood, and the executive control system of the mind. Despite the difficulty in definition, many philosophers believe that there is a broadly shared underlying intuition about what _____ is.

    a. bias
    b. The Rise and Fall of the Christian Coalition
    c. Christopher Ruddy
    d. Consciousness

2. A _____, psychopharmaceutical, or psychotropic is a chemical substance that crosses the blood-brain barrier and acts primarily upon the central nervous system where it affects brain function, resulting in changes in perception, mood, consciousness, cognition, and behavior. These substances may be used recreationally, to purposefully alter one's consciousness, as entheogens, for ritual, spiritual, and/or shamanic purposes, as a tool for studying or augmenting the mind, or therapeutically as medication.

Because psychoactive substances bring about subjective changes in consciousness and mood that the user may find pleasant (e.g. euphoria) or advantageous (e.g. increased alertness), many psychoactive substances are abused, that is, used excessively, despite health risks or negative consequences.

    a. Psychoeducation
    b. Psychoactive drug
    c. Rational Living Therapy
    d. Saprof

3. As a legal concept, _____ is a procedure under the insolvency laws of a number of common law jurisdictions. It functions as a rescue mechanism for insolvent entities and allows them to carry on running their business. The process - an alternative to liquidation - is often known as going into _____.

    a. Auxilium curiae
    b. Administration
    c. Order to show cause
    d. Antonio Commisso

4. . _____ is a 1922 British crime film directed by Graham Cutts and starring Hilda Bayley, Flora Le Breton, Ward McAllister and Cyril Raymond. A melodrama - it depicts the distribution of _____ by gangsters through a series of London nightclubs and the revenge sought by a man after the death of his daughter.

Because of its depiction of drug use, it was the most controversial British film of the 1920s.

    a. Deadlock
    b. Cocaine
    c. The Flying Scot

1. Drug Use: An Overview

5. _____ is a psychostimulant of the phenethylamine and amphetamine class of drugs. It increases alertness, concentration, energy, and in high doses, can induce euphoria, enhances self-esteem, and increase libido. _____ has high potential for abuse and addiction by activating the psychological reward system via triggering a cascading release of dopamine and norepinephrine in the brain.

   a. Psilocybin
   b. Visa overstay
   c. Methamphetamine
   d. Carmelo Barbaro

ANSWER KEY
1. Drug Use: An Overview

1. d
2. b
3. b
4. b
5. c

You can take the complete Chapter Practice Test

for 1. Drug Use: An Overview
on all key terms, persons, places, and concepts.

Online 99 Cents

http://www.epub4.1.22005.1.cram101.com/

Use www.Cram101.com for all your study needs

including Cram101's online interactive problem solving labs in

chemistry, statistics, mathematics, and more.

2. Drug Use as a Social Problem

CHAPTER OUTLINE: KEY TERMS, PEOPLE, PLACES, CONCEPTS

	Laissez-faire
	Social influence
	Social issue
	Homeland security
	Categories
	Drug user
	Psilocybin
	Public safety
	Substance abuse
	Drug Recognition Expert
	Nystagmus
	Benzedrine
	Hydrocodone
	Oxycodone
	Prescription
	Mental disorder
	Amphetamine
	Habituation
	Substance-related disorder
	Phoenix House
	Physical dependence

Cocaine

Psychological dependence

Substance dependence

Reinforcement

War on Drugs

Addictive personality

Controlled substance

Impulsivity

Agent

Alcohol dependence

Analogy

Dysfunctional family

Binge drinking

Punishment

Laissez-faire	In economics, laissez-faire describes an environment in which transactions between private parties are free from state intervention, including restrictive regulations, taxes, tariffs and enforced monopolies.
	The phrase laissez-faire is French and literally means 'let do', but it broadly implies 'let it be', or 'leave it alone.'
	Origins of the phrase
	According to historical legend, the phrase stems from a meeting in about 1680 between the powerful French finance minister Jean-Baptiste Colbert and a group of French businessmen led by a certain M. Le Gendre. When the eager mercantilist minister asked how the French state could be of service to the merchants and help promote their commerce, Le Gendre replied simply 'Laissez-nous faire' ('Leave us be', lit.
Social influence	Social influence occurs when one's emotions, opinions, or behaviors are affected by others. Social influence takes many forms and can be seen in conformity, socialization, peer pressure, obedience, leadership, persuasion, sales, and marketing. In 1958, Harvard psychologist, Herbert Kelman identified three broad varieties of social influence.
Social issue	A social issue (also called a social ill or a social problem) is a controversial issue that relates to people's personal lives and interactions. Social issues are distinguished from economic issues. Some issues have both social and economic aspects, such as immigration.
Homeland security	Homeland security is an umbrella term for security efforts to protect states against terrorist activity. Specifically, is a concerted national effort to prevent terrorist attacks within the U.S., reduce America's vulnerability to terrorism, and minimize the damage and recover from attacks that do occur.
	The term arose following a reorganization of many U.S. government agencies in 2003 to form the United States Department of Homeland Security after the September 11 attacks, and may be used to refer to the actions of that department, the United States Senate Committee on Homeland Security and Governmental Affairs, or the United States House of Representatives Committee on Homeland Security.
Categories	On May 14, 1867, the 27-year-old Charles Sanders Peirce, who eventually founded Pragmatism, presented a paper entitled 'On a New List of Categories' to the American Academy of Arts and Sciences. Among other things, this paper outlined a theory of predication involving three universal categories that Peirce continued to apply in philosophy and elsewhere for the rest of his life.

2. Drug Use as a Social Problem

Drug user	A drug user is a person who uses drugs either legally or illegally. The term user is typically employed more to refer to illegal drug use by a person who is often part of a subculture of recreational drug use. Drug users are often referred to as 'heads', depending on the drug used, i.e., pothead, hophead, crackhead, etc.
Psilocybin	Psilocybin is a naturally occurring psychedelic compound produced by over 200 species of mushrooms, collectively known as psilocybin mushrooms. The most potent are members of the genus Psilocybe, such as P. azurescens, P. semilanceata, and P. cyanescens, but psilocybin has also been isolated from about a dozen other genera. As a prodrug, psilocybin is quickly converted by the body to psilocin, which has mind-altering effects similar to those of LSD and mescaline.
Public safety	Public safety involves the prevention of and protection from events that could endanger the safety of the general public from significant danger, injury/harm, or damage, such as crimes or disasters (natural or man-made).
Substance abuse	Substance abuse, also known as drug abuse, is a patterned use of a substance (drug) in which the user consumes the substance in amounts or with methods neither approved nor supervised by medical professionals. Substance abuse/drug abuse is not limited to mood-altering or psycho-active drugs. If an activity is performed using the objects against the rules and policies of the matter (as in steroids for performance enhancement in sports), it is also called substance abuse.
Drug Recognition Expert	Drug Recognition Expert police officers are trained to be able to identify drug impaired drivers. DRE refers not only to the officers themselves, but to the 12-step procedure that these officers use. DRE was developed by police officers from the Los Angeles (California) Police Department.
Nystagmus	Nystagmus is a condition of involuntary eye movement, acquired in infancy or later in life, that may result in reduced or limited vision. There are two key forms of Nystagmus: pathological and physiological, with variations within each type. Nystagmus may be caused by congenital disorders, acquired or central nervous system disorders, toxicity, pharmaceutical drugs or alcohol.
Benzedrine	Benzedrine is the trade name of the racemic mixture of amphetamine (dl-amphetamine). It was marketed under this brandname in the USA by Smith, Kline & French in the form of inhalers, starting in 1928. Benzedrine was used to enlarge nasal and bronchial passages and it is closely related to other stimulants produced later, such as dextroamphetamine (d-amphetamine) and methamphetamine. Benzedrine should not be confused with the fundamentally different substance benzphetamine.
Hydrocodone	Hydrocodone is a semi-synthetic opioid derived from either of two naturally occurring opiates-- codeine and thebaine. Hydrocodone is an orally active narcotic analgesic (pain reliever) and antitussive (cough suppressant).

Oxycodone	Oxycodone is an analgesic medication synthesized from poppy-derived thebaine. It was developed in 1916 in Germany, as one of several new semi-synthetic opioids in an attempt to improve on the existing opioids: morphine, diacetylmorphine (heroin), and codeine. Oxycodone oral medications are generally prescribed for the relief of moderate to severe pain. Currently it is formulated as single ingredient products or compounded products. Some common examples of compounding are oxycodone with acetaminophen/paracetamol or non-steroidal anti-inflammatory drugs such as ibuprofen. The formulations are available as generics but are also made under various brand names. OxyContin is Purdue Pharma's brand for time-release oral oxycodone.
Prescription	In law, prescription is the method of sovereignty transfer of a territory through international law analogous to the common law doctrine of adverse possession for private real-estate. Prescription involves the open encroachment by the new sovereign upon the territory in question for a prolonged period of time, acting as the sovereign, without protest or other contest by the original sovereign. This doctrine legalizes de jure the de facto transfer of sovereignty caused in part by the original sovereign's extended negligence and/or neglect of the area in question.
Mental disorder	A mental disorder or mental illness is a psychological pattern or anomaly, potentially reflected in behavior, that is generally associated with distress or disability, and which is not considered part of normal development of a person's culture. Mental disorders are generally defined by a combination of how a person feels, acts, thinks or perceives. This may be associated with particular regions or functions of the brain or rest of the nervous system, often in a social context.
Amphetamine	Amphetamine or amfetamine (INN) is a psychostimulant drug of the phenethylamine class which produces increased wakefulness and focus in association with decreased fatigue and appetite. Brand names of medications that contain, or metabolize into, amphetamine include Adderall, Dexedrine, Dextrostat, Desoxyn, ProCentra, and Vyvanse, as well as Benzedrine in the past. The drug is also used recreationally and as a performance enhancer.
Habituation	Habituation can be defined as a process or as a procedure. As a process it is defined as a decrease in an elicited behavior resulting from the repeated presentation of an eliciting stimulus (a simple form of learning). As a procedure it is defined as the repeated presentation of an eliciting stimulus that may result in the decline of the elicited behavior (the process of habituation), an increase of the elicited behavior (the process of sensitization), or an initial increase followed by a decline of the elicited behavior (a sensitization process followed by a habituation process).

2. Drug Use as a Social Problem

Phoenix House	Phoenix House is a nonprofit drug and alcohol rehabilitation organization operating in ten states with 150 programs. Programs serve individuals, families, and communities affected by substance abuse and dependency.
	Phoenix House was founded in 1967 by six heroin addicts who met at a detoxification program in a New York hospital.
Physical dependence	Physical dependence refers to a state resulting from chronic use of a drug that has produced tolerance and where negative physical symptoms of withdrawal result from abrupt discontinuation or dosage reduction. Physical dependence can develop from low-dose therapeutic use of certain medications such as benzodiazepines, opioids, antiepileptics and antidepressants, as well as misuse of recreational drugs such as alcohol, opioids and benzodiazepines. The higher the dose used, the greater the duration of use, and the earlier age use began are predictive of worsened physical dependence and thus more severe withdrawal syndromes.
Cocaine	Cocaine is a 1922 British crime film directed by Graham Cutts and starring Hilda Bayley, Flora Le Breton, Ward McAllister and Cyril Raymond. A melodrama - it depicts the distribution of cocaine by gangsters through a series of London nightclubs and the revenge sought by a man after the death of his daughter.
	Because of its depiction of drug use, it was the most controversial British film of the 1920s.
Psychological dependence	In the APA Dictionary of Psychology, psychological dependence is defined as 'dependence on a psychoactive substance for the reinforcement it provides.' Most times psychological dependence is classified under addiction. They are similar in that addiction is a physiological 'craving' for something and psychological dependence is a 'need' for a particular substance because it causes enjoyable mental affects.
	A person becomes dependent on something to help alleviate specific emotions.
Substance dependence	Substance dependence, commonly called drug addiction is defined as a drug user's compulsive need to use controlled substances in order to function normally. When such substances are unobtainable, the user suffers from substance withdrawal.
	The section about substance dependence in the Diagnostic and Statistical Manual of Mental Disorders (more specifically, the 2000 'text revision', the DSM-IV-TR) does not use the word addiction at all.

Reinforcement	Reinforcement is a term in operant conditioning and behavior analysis for a process of strengthening a directly measurable dimension of behavior-such as rate (e.g., pulling a lever more frequently), duration (e.g., pulling a lever for longer periods of time), magnitude (e.g., pulling a lever with greater force), or latency (e.g., pulling a lever more quickly following the onset of an environmental event)-as a function of the delivery of a stimulus (e.g. money from a slot machine) immediately or shortly after the occurrence of the behavior. Giving a monkey a banana for performing a trick is an example of positive reinforcement. Reinforcement is only said to have occurred if the delivery of the stimulus is directly caused by the response made.
War on Drugs	The War on Drugs is a controversial campaign of prohibition and foreign military aid and military intervention being undertaken by the United States government, with the assistance of participating countries, intended to both define and reduce the illegal drug trade. This initiative includes a set of drug policies of the United States that are intended to discourage the production, distribution, and consumption of illegal psychoactive drugs. The term 'War on Drugs' was first used by President Richard Nixon in 1971.
Addictive personality	An addictive personality refers to a particuar set of personality traits that make an individual predisposed to addictions. People who are substance dependent are characterized by: a physical or psychological dependency that negatively impacts the quality of life. They are frequently connected with substance abuse; however, people with addictive personalities are also highly at risk of becoming addicted to gambling, food, pornography, exercise, work, and codependency.
Controlled substance	A controlled substance is generally a drug or chemical whose manufacture, possession, and use are regulated by a government. This may include illegal drugs and prescription medications (designated Controlled Drug in the United Kingdom).
Impulsivity	Impulsivity is a personality trait characterized by the inclination of an individual to initiate behavior without adequate forethought as to the consequences of their actions, acting on the spur of the moment. Eysenck and Eysenck related impulsivity to risk-taking, lack of planning, and making up one's mind quickly. Impulsivity has been shown to be a major component of various neuropsychiatric disorders such as ADHD, substance abuse disorders and bipolar disorder.
Agent	In economics, an agent is an actor and decision maker in a model. Typically, every agent makes decisions by solving a well or ill defined optimization/choice problem. The term agent can also be seen as equivalent to player in game theory.
Alcohol dependence	Alcohol dependence is a psychiatric diagnosis (a substance related disorder DSM-IV) describing an entity in which an individual uses alcohol despite significant areas of dysfunction, evidence of physical dependence, and/or related hardship, and also may cause stress and bipolar disorder.

2. Drug Use as a Social Problem

According to the DSM-IV criteria for alcohol dependence, at least three out of seven of the following criteria must be manifest during a 12 month period:•Tolerance•Withdrawal symptoms or clinically defined Alcohol Withdrawal Syndrome•Use in larger amounts or for longer periods than intended•Persistent desire or unsuccessful efforts to cut down on alcohol use•Time is spent obtaining alcohol or recovering from effects•Social, occupational and recreational pursuits are given up or reduced because of alcohol use•Use is continued despite knowledge of alcohol-related harm (physical or psychological)History and epidemiology

About 12% of American adults have had an alcohol dependence problem at some time in their life. The term 'alcohol dependence' has replaced 'alcoholism' as a term in order that individuals do not internalize the idea of cure and disease, but can approach alcohol as a chemical they may depend upon to cope with outside pressures.

Analogy	Analogy is a cognitive process of transferring information or meaning from a particular subject (the analogue or source) to another particular subject (the target), and a linguistic expression corresponding to such a process. In a narrower sense, analogy is an inference or an argument from one particular to another particular, as opposed to deduction, induction, and abduction, where at least one of the premises or the conclusion is general. The word analogy can also refer to the relation between the source and the target themselves, which is often, though not necessarily, a similarity, as in the biological notion of analogy.
Dysfunctional family	A dysfunctional family is a family in which conflict, misbehavior, and often abuse on the part of individual members occur continually and regularly, leading other members to accommodate such actions. Children sometimes grow up in such families with the understanding that such an arrangement is normal. Dysfunctional families are primarily a result of co-dependent adults, and may also be affected by addictions, such as substance abuse (alcohol, drugs, etc)..
Binge drinking	Binge drinking is the modern epithet for drinking alcoholic beverages with the primary intention of becoming intoxicated by heavy consumption of alcohol over a short period of time. It is a kind of purposeful drinking style that is popular in several countries worldwide, and overlaps somewhat with social drinking since it is often done in groups. The degree of intoxication, however, varies between and within various cultures that engage in this practice.
Punishment	In operant conditioning, punishment is any change in a human or animal's surroundings that occurs after a given behavior or response which reduces the likelihood of that behavior occurring again in the future. As with reinforcement, it is the behavior, not the animal, that is punished. Whether a change is or is not punishing is only known by its effect on the rate of the behavior, not by any 'hostile' or aversive features of the change.

1. A _____ is a person who uses drugs either legally or illegally. The term user is typically employed more to refer to illegal drug use by a person who is often part of a subculture of recreational drug use. _____s are often referred to as 'heads', depending on the drug used, i.e., pothead, hophead, crackhead, etc.

   a. Drug user
   b. Malawi Gold
   c. Maritime Analysis and Operations Centre
   d. Midnight Express

2. _____ is a 1922 British crime film directed by Graham Cutts and starring Hilda Bayley, Flora Le Breton, Ward McAllister and Cyril Raymond. A melodrama - it depicts the distribution of _____ by gangsters through a series of London nightclubs and the revenge sought by a man after the death of his daughter.

   Because of its depiction of drug use, it was the most controversial British film of the 1920s.

   a. Deadlock
   b. The Embezzler
   c. The Flying Scot
   d. Cocaine

3. An _____ refers to a particuar set of personality traits that make an individual predisposed to addictions. People who are substance dependent are characterized by: a physical or psychological dependency that negatively impacts the quality of life. They are frequently connected with substance abuse; however, people with _____(ies) are also highly at risk of becoming addicted to gambling, food, pornography, exercise, work, and codependency.

   a. Addictive personality
   b. Depressive personality disorder
   c. Joan Lachkar
   d. Personality development disorder

4. _____ is the modern epithet for drinking alcoholic beverages with the primary intention of becoming intoxicated by heavy consumption of alcohol over a short period of time. It is a kind of purposeful drinking style that is popular in several countries worldwide, and overlaps somewhat with social drinking since it is often done in groups. The degree of intoxication, however, varies between and within various cultures that engage in this practice.

   a. Binge drinking
   b. Beer mile
   c. Centurion
   d. Kastenlauf

5. . In economics, _____ describes an environment in which transactions between private parties are free from state intervention, including restrictive regulations, taxes, tariffs and enforced monopolies.

2. Drug Use as a Social Problem

The phrase _____ is French and literally means 'let do', but it broadly implies 'let it be', or 'leave it alone.'

Origins of the phrase

According to historical legend, the phrase stems from a meeting in about 1680 between the powerful French finance minister Jean-Baptiste Colbert and a group of French businessmen led by a certain M. Le Gendre. When the eager mercantilist minister asked how the French state could be of service to the merchants and help promote their commerce, Le Gendre replied simply 'Laissez-nous faire' ('Leave us be', lit.

a. London Co-operative Society
b. Market fundamentalism
c. Laissez-faire
d. Means of labor

1. a
2. d
3. a
4. a
5. c

You can take the complete Chapter Practice Test

for 2. Drug Use as a Social Problem
on all key terms, persons, places, and concepts.

Online 99 Cents

http://www.epub4.1.22005.2.cram101.com/

Use www.Cram101.com for all your study needs

including Cram101's online interactive problem solving labs in

chemistry, statistics, mathematics, and more.

	Criminalization
	Reformism
	Distribution
	International trade
	Patent medicine
	Methamphetamine
	Cosmetics
	Orphan drug
	Controlled substance
	Narcotic
	Prescription
	J. Edgar Hoover
	Drug user
	Federal prison
	Prison
	Agent
	Substance abuse
	Drug possession
	Introduction
	Popularity
	Controlled Substances Act

Diversion

Drug prohibition law

Categories

Alcohol dependence

Uniform Controlled Substances Act

Screening

Hypothetico-deductive model

Border guard

Customs

National park

Ronald Reagan

Costs

Drug education

Consciousness

Criminalization	Criminalization, in criminology, is 'the process by which behaviors and individuals are transformed into crime and criminals'. Previously legal acts may be transformed into crimes by legislation or judicial decision. However, there is usually a formal presumption in the rules of statutory interpretation against the retrospective application of laws and only the use of express words by the legislature may rebut this presumption.
Reformism	Reformism is the belief that gradual changes through and within existing institutions of a society can ultimately change a society's fundamental economic relations, economic system, and political structures. This belief grew out of opposition to revolutionary socialism, which contends that revolutions are necessary for fundamental structural changes to occur. Socialist reformism, or evolutionary socialism, was first put forward by Eduard Bernstein, a leading social democrat.
Distribution	Distribution in economics refers to the way total output, income, or wealth is distributed among individuals or among the factors of production (such as labour, land, and capital).. In general theory and the national income and product accounts, each unit of output corresponds to a unit of income. One use of national accounts is for classifying factor incomes and measuring their respective shares, as in National Income.
International trade	International trade is the exchange of capital, goods, and services across international borders or territories. In most countries, such trade represents a significant share of gross domestic product (GDP). While international trade has been present throughout much of history, its economic, social, and political importance has been on the rise in recent centuries.
Patent medicine	Patent medicine refers to medical compounds of questionable effectiveness sold under a variety of names and labels. The term 'patent medicine' is somewhat of a misnomer because, in most cases, although many of the products were trademarked, they were never patented (most avoided the patent process so as not to reveal products' often hazardous and questionable ingredients). Perhaps the only 'patent medicine' ever to be patented was Castoria.
Methamphetamine	Methamphetamine is a psychostimulant of the phenethylamine and amphetamine class of drugs. It increases alertness, concentration, energy, and in high doses, can induce euphoria, enhances self-esteem, and increase libido. Methamphetamine has high potential for abuse and addiction by activating the psychological reward system via triggering a cascading release of dopamine and norepinephrine in the brain.
Cosmetics	Cosmetics are substances used to enhance the appearance or odor of the human body. Cosmetics include skin-care creams, lotions, powders, perfumes, lipsticks, fingernail and toe nail polish, eye and facial makeup, towelettes, permanent waves, colored contact lenses, hair colors, hair sprays and gels, deodorants, hand sanitizer, baby products, bath oils, bubble baths, bath salts, butters and many other types of products.

3. Drug Policy

Orphan drug	An orphan drug is a pharmaceutical agent that has been developed specifically to treat a rare medical condition, the condition itself being referred to as an orphan disease. The assignment of orphan status to a disease and to any drugs developed to treat it is a matter of public policy in many countries, and has resulted in medical breakthroughs that may not have otherwise been achieved due to the economics of drug research and development. In the US and EU it is easier to gain marketing approval for an orphan drug, and there may be other financial incentives such as extended exclusivity periods.
Controlled substance	A controlled substance is generally a drug or chemical whose manufacture, possession, and use are regulated by a government. This may include illegal drugs and prescription medications (designated Controlled Drug in the United Kingdom).
Narcotic	The term narcotic originally referred medically to any psychoactive compound with sleep-inducing properties. In the United States of America it has since become associated with opioids, commonly morphine and heroin. The term is, today, imprecisely defined and typically has negative connotations.
Prescription	In law, prescription is the method of sovereignty transfer of a territory through international law analogous to the common law doctrine of adverse possession for private real-estate. Prescription involves the open encroachment by the new sovereign upon the territory in question for a prolonged period of time, acting as the sovereign, without protest or other contest by the original sovereign. This doctrine legalizes de jure the de facto transfer of sovereignty caused in part by the original sovereign's extended negligence and/or neglect of the area in question.
J. Edgar Hoover	John Edgar Hoover (January 1, 1895 - May 2, 1972) was the first Director of the Federal Bureau of Investigation (FBI) of the United States. Appointed director of the Bureau of Investigation--predecessor to the FBI--in 1924, he was instrumental in founding the FBI in 1935, where he remained director until his death in 1972. Hoover is credited with building the FBI into a large and efficient crime-fighting agency, and with instituting a number of modernizations to police technology, such as a centralized fingerprint file and forensic laboratories.

Late in life and after his death Hoover became a controversial figure as evidence of his secretive actions became public. His critics have accused him of exceeding the jurisdiction of the FBI. He used the FBI to harass political dissenters and activists, to amass secret files on political leaders, and to collect evidence using illegal methods. FBI directors are now limited to one 10-year term, subject to extension by the United States Senate, because of his long and controversial tenure. Early life and education

J. Edgar Hoover was born on New Year's Day 1895 in Washington, D.C., to Anna Marie (née Scheitlin; 1860-1938), who was of German Swiss descent, and Dickerson Naylor Hoover, Sr. (1856 -1921), of English and German ancestry. The uncle of Hoover's mother was a Swiss honorary consul general to the United States. |

Hoover grew up near the Eastern Market in Washington's Capitol Hill neighborhood. At Central High, he sang in the school choir, participated in the Reserve Officers' Training Corps program, and competed on the debate team. He obtained a law degree from George Washington University in 1916, and an LLM, a Master of Laws degree, in 1917 from the same university. While a law student, Hoover became interested in the career of Anthony Comstock, the New York City United States Postal Inspector, who waged prolonged campaigns against fraud and vice, and also was against pornography and birth control. FBI career

During World War I, immediately after getting his LLM, Hoover was hired by the Justice Department. He was soon promoted to head of the Enemy Aliens Registration Section. In August 1919, he became head of the new General Intelligence Division of the Bureau of Investigation within the Justice Department . From there, in 1921, he rose in the Bureau of Investigation to deputy head, and in 1924, the Attorney General made him the acting director. On May 10, 1924, President Calvin Coolidge appointed Hoover as the sixth director of the Bureau of Investigation, following President Warren Harding's death and in response to allegations that the prior director, William J. Burns, was involved in the Teapot Dome scandal. When Hoover took over the Bureau of Investigation, it had approximately 650 employees, including 441 Special Agents.

Hoover was noted as sometimes being capricious in his leadership; he frequently fired FBI agents, singling out those who he thought 'looked stupid like truck drivers' or he considered to be 'pinheads'. He also relocated agents who had displeased him to career-ending assignments and locations. Melvin Purvis was a prime example; he was one of the most effective agents in capturing and breaking up 1930s gangs and received substantial public recognition, but a jealous Hoover maneuvered him out of the FBI.

Hoover often hailed local law-enforcement officers around the country and built up a national network of supporters and admirers in the process. One that he often commended was the conservative sheriff of Caddo Parish, Louisiana, J. Howell Flournoy, for particular effectiveness. Gangster wars

In the early 1930s, criminal gangs carried out large numbers of bank robberies in the Midwest. They used their superior firepower and fast getaway cars to elude local law enforcement agencies and avoid arrest. Many of these criminals, particularly John Dillinger, who became famous for leaping over bank cages and repeatedly escaping from jails and police traps, frequently made newspaper headlines across the United States. Since the robbers operated across state lines, their crimes became federal offenses, giving Hoover and his men the authority to pursue them. Initially, the FBI suffered some embarrassing foul-ups, in particular with Dillinger and his conspirators. A raid on a summer lodge named 'Little Bohemia' in Manitowish Waters, Wisconsin, left an FBI agent and a civilian bystander dead, and others wounded. All the gangsters escaped. Hoover realized that his job was now on the line, and he pulled out all stops to capture the culprits.

3. Drug Policy

In late July 1934, Special Agent Melvin Purvis, the Director of Operations in the Chicago office, received a tip on Dillinger's whereabouts which paid off when Dillinger was located, ambushed and killed by FBI agents outside the Biograph Theater.

In the same period, there were numerous Mafia shootings as a result of Prohibition, while Hoover continued to deny the very existence of organized crime. Frank Costello helped encourage this view by feeding Hoover, 'an inveterate horseplayer' known to send Special Agents to place $100 bets for him, tips on sure winners through their mutual friend, gossip columnist Walter Winchell. Hoover said the Bureau had 'much more important functions' than arresting bookmakers and gamblers.

Even though he was not there, Hoover was credited with several highly publicized captures or shootings of outlaws and bank robbers. These included that of Dillinger, Alvin Karpis, and Machine Gun Kelly, which led to the Bureau's powers being broadened and it was given its new name in 1935: the Federal Bureau of Investigation. In 1939, the FBI became pre-eminent in the field of domestic intelligence. Hoover made changes, such as expanding and combining fingerprint files in the Identification Division to compile the largest collection of fingerprints to date. Hoover also helped to expand the FBI's recruitment and create the FBI Laboratory, a division established in 1932 to examine evidence found by the FBI.Investigation of subversion and radicals

Hoover was concerned about subversion, and under his leadership, the FBI spied upon tens of thousands of suspected subversives and radicals. According to critics, Hoover tended to exaggerate the dangers of these alleged subversives and many times overstepped his bounds in his pursuit of eliminating that perceived threat.

The FBI investigated rings of German saboteurs and spies starting in the late 1930s, and had primary responsibility for counterespionage. The first arrests of German agents were made in 1938, and continued throughout World War II. In the Quirin affair during World War II, German U-boats set two small groups of Nazi agents ashore in Florida and Long Island to cause acts of sabotage within the country. The two teams were apprehended after one of the men contacted the FBI, and told them everything. He was also charged and convicted. President Harry Truman wrote in his memoirs: 'The country had reason to be proud of and have confidence in our security agencies. They had kept us almost totally free of sabotage and espionage during World War II'.

The FBI participated in the Venona Project, a pre-World War II joint project with the British to eavesdrop on Soviet spies in the UK and the United States. It was not initially realized that espionage was being committed, but due to multiple wartime Soviet use of one-time pad ciphers, which are normally unbreakable, redundancies were created, enabling some intercepts to be decoded, which established the espionage. Hoover kept the intercepts--America's greatest counterintelligence secret--in a locked safe in his office, choosing not to inform President Truman, Attorney General J. Howard McGrath, or two Secretaries of State--Dean Acheson and General George Marshall--while they held office.

He informed the Central Intelligence Agency (CIA) of the Venona Project in 1952.

In 1946, U.S. Attorney General Tom C. Clark authorized Hoover to compile a list of potentially disloyal Americans who might be detained during a wartime national emergency. In 1950, at the outbreak of the Korean War, Hoover submitted to President Truman a plan to suspend the writ of habeas corpus and detain 12,000 Americans suspected of disloyalty. Truman did not act on the plan. COINTELPRO years

In 1956, Hoover was becoming increasingly frustrated by Supreme Court decisions that limited the Justice Department's ability to prosecute people for their political opinions, most notably communists. At this time he formalized a covert 'dirty tricks' program under the name COINTELPRO.

This program remained in place until it was revealed to the public in 1971, after the theft of many internal documents stolen from an office in Media, Pennsylvania, and was the cause of some of the harshest criticism of Hoover and the FBI. COINTELPRO was first used to disrupt the Communist Party, where Hoover went after targets that ranged from suspected everyday spies to larger celebrity figures such as Charlie Chaplin who were seen as spreading Communist Party propaganda, and later organizations such as the Black Panther Party, Martin Luther King, Jr.'s SCLC and others. Its methods included infiltration, burglaries, illegal wiretaps, planting forged documents and spreading false rumors about key members of target organizations. Some authors have charged that COINTELPRO methods also included inciting violence and arranging murders. In 1975, the activities of COINTELPRO were investigated by the 'United States Senate Select Committee to Study Governmental Operations with Respect to Intelligence Activities' called the Church Committee after its chairman, Senator Frank Church (D-Idaho) and these activities were declared illegal and contrary to the Constitution. Hoover amassed significant power by collecting files containing large amounts of compromising and potentially embarrassing information on many powerful people, especially politicians. According to Laurence Silberman, appointed Deputy Attorney General in early 1974, FBI Director Clarence M. Kelley thought such files either did not exist or had been destroyed. After The Washington Post broke a story in January 1975, Kelley searched and found them in his outer office. The House Judiciary Committee then demanded that Silberman testify about them.

In 1956, several years before he targeted King, Hoover had a public showdown with T.R.M. Howard, a civil rights leader from Mound Bayou, Mississippi. During a national speaking tour, Howard had criticized the FBI's failure to thoroughly investigate the racially motivated murders of George W. Lee, Lamar Smith, and Emmett Till. Hoover wrote an open letter to the press singling out these statements as 'irresponsible.'Response to Mafia and civil rights groups

In the 1950s, evidence of Hoover's unwillingness to focus FBI resources on the Mafia became grist for the media and his many detractors.

3. Drug Policy

His moves against people who maintained contacts with subversive elements, some of whom were members of the civil rights movement, also led to accusations of trying to undermine their reputations. The treatment of Martin Luther King, Jr. and actress Jean Seberg are two examples. Jacqueline Kennedy recalled that Hoover told President Kennedy that King tried to arrange a sex party while in the capital for the March on Washington and told Robert Kennedy that King made derogatory comments during the President's funeral.

Hoover personally directed the FBI investigation into the assassination of President John F. Kennedy. In 1964, just days before Hoover testified in the earliest stages of the Warren Commission hearings, President Lyndon B. Johnson waived the then mandatory U.S. Government Service Retirement Age of seventy, allowing Hoover to remain the FBI Director 'for life.' The House Select Committee on Assassinations issued a report in 1979 critical of the performance by the FBI, the Warren Commission, and other agencies. The report also criticized what it characterized as the FBI's reluctance to thoroughly investigate the possibility of a conspiracy to assassinate the President. Late career and death

Presidents Harry S. Truman and John F. Kennedy each considered dismissing Hoover as FBI Director, but ultimately concluded that the political cost of doing so would be too great.

Hoover's FBI investigated Hollywood lobbyist Jack Valenti, a special assistant and confidant to President Lyndon Johnson, in 1964. Despite Valenti's two-year marriage to Johnson's personal secretary, the investigation focused on rumors that he was having a gay relationship with a commercial photographer friend.

Hoover maintained strong support in Congress until his death at his Washington, D.C., home on May 2, 1972, from a heart attack attributed to cardio-vascular disease. His body lay in state in the Rotunda of the U.S. Capitol, where Chief Justice Warren Burger eulogized him. President Nixon delivered another eulogy at the funeral service in the National Presbyterian Church. In public, Nixon said 'One of the giants... a national symbol of courage, patriotism and granite-like honesty and integrity.' In private, Nixon's reaction was 'That old cocksucker'. Hoover was buried in the Congressional Cemetery in Washington, D.C., next to the graves of his parents and a sister who died in infancy.

Operational command of the Bureau passed to Associate Director Clyde Tolson. On May 3, Nixon appointed L. Patrick Gray, a Justice Department official with no FBI experience, as Acting Director, with W. Mark Felt remaining as Associate Director. Legacy

Hoover was a consultant to Warner Bros. on a 1959 theatrical film about the FBI, The FBI Story, and in 1965 on Warner Bros.' long-running spin-off television series, The F.B.I. Hoover personally made sure that Warner Bros. would portray the FBI more favorably than other crime dramas of the times.

In 1979, there was a large increase in conflict in the House Select Committee on Assassinations (HSCA) under Senator Richard Schweiker, which had re-opened the investigation into the assassination of President Kennedy, reported that Hoover's FBI 'failed to investigate adequately the possibility of a conspiracy to assassinate the President'. The HSCA further reported that Hoover's FBI 'was deficient in its sharing of information with other agencies and departments'.

The FBI Headquarters in Washington. Because of the controversial nature of Hoover's legacy, there have been periodic proposals to rename it by legislation proposed by both Republicans and Democrats in the House and Senate. In 2001, Senator Harry Reid sponsored an amendment to strip Hoover's name from the building. 'J. Edgar Hoover's name on the FBI building is a stain on the building', Reid said. However, the Senate never adopted the amendment. Personal life

Since the 1940s, rumors have circulated that Hoover was gay. It has been suggested that Clyde Tolson, an associate director of the FBI who was Hoover's heir, may have been his lover.

Hoover hunted down and threatened anyone who made insinuations about his sexuality. He also spread unsubstantiated rumors that Adlai Stevenson was gay to damage the liberal governor's 1952 presidential campaign. His extensive secret files contained surveillance material on Eleanor Roosevelt's alleged lesbian lovers, speculated to be acquired for the purpose of blackmail.

Some authors have dismissed the rumors about Hoover's sexuality and his relationship with Tolson in particular as unlikely, while others have described them as probable or even 'confirmed', and still others have reported the rumors without stating an opinion. Hoover described Tolson as his alter ego: the men not only worked closely together during the day but also took meals, went to night clubs and vacationed together. This closeness between the two men is often cited as evidence that they were lovers, though some FBI employees who knew them, such as W. Mark Felt, say that the relationship was merely 'brotherly.' However, former FBI official Mike Mason suggested that some of Hoover's colleagues were denying he had a sexual relationship with Tolson in an effort to protect his image.

Tolson inherited Hoover's estate and moved into his home, having accepted the American flag that draped Hoover's casket. Tolson is buried a few yards away from Hoover in the Congressional Cemetery.

Among those skeptical of claims that Hoover was homosexual is Hoover's biographer Richard Hack. Hack notes that Hoover was romantically linked to actress Dorothy Lamour in the late 1930s and early 1940s, and that after Hoover's death Lamour did not deny rumors that she had had an affair with Hoover in the years between her two marriages. Hack additionally reports that during the 1940s and 1950s, Hoover so often attended social events with Lela Rogers, the divorced mother of dancer and actress Ginger Rogers, that many of their mutual friends assumed the pair would eventually marry.

3. Drug Policy

In his 1993 biography Official and Confidential: The Secret Life of J. Edgar Hoover, journalist Anthony Summers quoted 'society divorcee' Susan Rosenstiel as claiming to have seen Hoover engaging in cross-dressing in the 1950s. She stated that on two occasions she witnessed Hoover wearing a fluffy pink dress with flounces and lace, stockings, high heels and a black curly wig, at homosexual orgies:'

In 1958 the bisexual millionaire distiller and philanthropist Lewis Solon Rosenstiel asked Susan Rosenstiel, his fourth wife, if -- having been previously married to another bisexual man for nine years -- she had ever seen 'a homosexual orgy'. Although she had once surprised her sixty-eight-year-old husband in bed with his attorney, Roy Cohn, Susan told Summers that she had never before been invited to view sex between men. With her consent, the couple went one day, soon after this odd question, to Manhattan's Plaza Hotel. Cohn, a former aide to Senator Joseph McCarthy and a Republican power broker, met them at the door. As she and her husband entered the suite, 'Susan said, she recognized a third man: J. Edgar Hoover', director of the Federal Bureau of Investigation (FBI), whom she had met previously at her New York City Upper East Side townhouse. Hoover, Lewis had explained, gave him access to influential politicians; he returned these favors, in part, by paying the director's gambling debts. '

Summers also said that the Mafia had blackmail material on Hoover, which made Hoover reluctant to aggressively pursue organized crime. Although never corroborated, the allegation of cross-dressing has been widely repeated. In the words of author Thomas Doherty, 'For American popular culture, the image of the zaftig FBI director as a Christine Jorgensen wanna-be was too delicious not to savor.' Skeptics of the cross-dressing story point to Susan Rosenstiel's poor credibility (she served time at Rikers Island jail for perjuring herself in a 1971 case) and say recklessly indiscreet behavior by Hoover would have been totally out of character, whatever his sexuality. Most biographers consider the story of Mafia blackmail to be unlikely in light of the FBI's investigations of the Mafia. Truman Capote, who helped spread salacious rumors about Hoover, once remarked that he was more interested in making Hoover angry than determining whether the rumors were true.

Attorney Roy Cohn, an associate of Hoover during the 1950s investigations of Communists and himself a closeted homosexual, opined that Hoover was too frightened of his own sexuality to have anything approaching a normal sexual or romantic relationship.

In his 2004 study of the Lavender Scare, historian David K. Johnson attacked the notion of Hoover's homosexuality for relying on 'the kind of tactics Hoover and the security program he oversaw perfected -- guilt by association, rumor, and unverified gossip.' He views Rosenstiel as a liar who was paid for her story, whose 'description of Hoover in drag engaging in sex with young blond boys in leather while desecrating the Bible is clearly a homophobic fantasy.' He believes only those who have forgotten the virulence of the decades-long campaign against homosexuals in government can believe reports that Hoover would allow himself to be seen in compromising situations.

Some people affiliated with Hoover, however, defended the claims that he had homosexual tendencies. Ethel Merman, a friend of Hoover since 1938, stated in 1978 'Some of my best friends are homosexual. Everybody knew about J. Edgar Hoover, but he was the best chief the FBI ever had.' Another FBI agent who had gone on fishing trips with Hoover and Tolson revealed that the director liked to 'sunbathe all day in the nude.' Hoover often frequented New York City's Stork Club and one observer -- soap model Luisa Stuart, who was 18 or 19 at the time -- told Summers she saw Hoover holding hands with Tolson as they all rode in a limo uptown to the Cotton Club in 1936.

Novelist William Styron told Summers that he once spotted Hoover and Tolson in a California beach house and the director was painting his friend's toenails. Harry Hay, founder of the Mattachine Society, one of the first gay rights organizations, confirmed that Hoover and Tolson sat in boxes owned by and used exclusively by gay men at their racing haunt Del Mar in California. One medical expert told Summers that Hoover was 'strongly predominant homosexual orientation' and another categorized him as a 'bisexual with failed heterosexuality.'Freemasonry

Hoover was a devoted Freemason, being raised a Master Mason on 9 November 1920, in Federal Lodge No. 1, Washington, DC, just two months before his 26th birthday. During his 52 years with the Masons, he received many medals, awards and decorations. Eventually in 1955, he was coroneted a Thirty-Third Degree Inspector General Honorary in the Southern Scottish Rite Jurisdiction. He was also awarded the Scottish Rite's highest recognition, the Grand Cross of Honor, in 1965. Today a J. Edgar Hoover room exists within the House of the Temple. The room contains many of Hoover's personal papers and records. Honors •In 1938, Oklahoma Baptist University awarded Hoover an honorary doctorate during commencement exercises at which he spoke.•In 1939, the National Academy of Sciences awarded Hoover its Public Welfare Medal.•In 1950, King George VI of the United Kingdom awarded Hoover an honorary knighthood in the Order of the British Empire.•In 1955, President Dwight Eisenhower gave Hoover the National Security Medal.•In 1966, President Lyndon B. Johnson bestowed the State Department's Distinguished Service Award on Hoover for his service as director of the FBI.•The FBI headquarters in Washington, D.C., is named the J. Edgar Hoover Building.•Congress voted to honour Hoover's memory by publishing a memorial book. J. Edgar Hoover: Memorial Tributes in the Congress of the United States and Various Articles and Editorials Relating to His Life and Work appeared in 1974.•In Schaumburg, Illinois. In 1994, after personal information about Hoover was released, the school's name was changed to reflect Herbert Hoover instead of J. Edgar Hoover.Portrayals

J. Edgar Hoover has been portrayed many times in film and on stage. Some notable portrayals include:•In the 1971 Woody Allen film Bananas, J. Edgar Hoover was portrayed by actress Dorothi Fox.•Broderick Crawford and James Wainwright portrayed Hoover in the Larry Cohen film The Private Files of J.

3. Drug Policy

Edgar Hoover.•Hoover was portrayed by actor Dolph Sweet in the TV miniseries King (1978).•Hoover was portrayed by actor Sheldon Leonard in the William Friedkin film The Brink's Job (1978).•Hoover was portrayed by actor Ernest Borgnine in the TV film Blood Feud (1983), as well as in Hoover (2000).•Hoover was portrayed by actor Vincent Gardenia in the TV film Kennedy (1983).•Hoover was portrayed by actor Jack Warden in the TV film Hoover vs. The Kennedys (1987).•Hoover was portrayed by actor Treat Williams in the TV film J. Edgar Hoover.•Hoover was portrayed by actor Kevin Dunn in the film Chaplin (1992).•Hoover was portrayed by actor Pat Hingle in the TV film Citizen Cohn (1992).•Hoover was portrayed by actor Richard Dysart, both in the TV film Marilyn & Bobby: Her Final Affair (1993) and in Mario Van Peebles' 1995 film Panther.•Hoover was portrayed by actor Bob Hoskins in the Oliver Stone drama Nixon (1995).•Hoover was portrayed by actor David Fredericks in two episodes of The X-Files, as well as on its sister show Millennium.•Hoover was portrayed by actor Kelsey Grammer with John Goodman as his lover, in the Harry Shearer comic musical J. Edgar! on L.A. Theatre Works' The Play's the Thing (2001).•Hoover was originally portrayed by Eric Jordan Young in the musical Dillinger, Public Enemy Number One.•Hoover was portrayed by actor Billy Crudup in the Michael Mann film Public Enemies (2009).•Hoover was portrayed by actor Enrico Colantoni in the TV miniseries The Kennedys (2011).•Hoover is portrayed by actor Leonardo DiCaprio in the Clint Eastwood biopic J. Edgar (2011)..

Drug user	A drug user is a person who uses drugs either legally or illegally. The term user is typically employed more to refer to illegal drug use by a person who is often part of a subculture of recreational drug use. Drug users are often referred to as 'heads', depending on the drug used, i.e., pothead, hophead, crackhead, etc.
Federal prison	Federal prisons are run by national governments in countries where subdivisions of the country also operate prisons. In the United States federal prisons are operated by the Federal Bureau of Prisons. In Canada the Correctional Service of Canada operates federal prisons.
Prison	Prison is a 1988 horror film starring Viggo Mortensen. It was filmed at the Old State Prison in Rawlins, Wyoming with many of its residents on the cast and crew. In 1956, inmate Charlie Forsythe swallowed 60,000 volts of electricity for a murder he did not commit.
Agent	In economics, an agent is an actor and decision maker in a model. Typically, every agent makes decisions by solving a well or ill defined optimization/choice problem. The term agent can also be seen as equivalent to player in game theory.

3. Drug Policy

Substance abuse	Substance abuse, also known as drug abuse, is a patterned use of a substance (drug) in which the user consumes the substance in amounts or with methods neither approved nor supervised by medical professionals. Substance abuse/drug abuse is not limited to mood-altering or psycho-active drugs. If an activity is performed using the objects against the rules and policies of the matter (as in steroids for performance enhancement in sports), it is also called substance abuse.
Drug possession	Drug possession is the crime of having one or more illegal drugs in one's possession, either for personal use, distribution, sale or otherwise. Illegal drugs fall into different categories and sentences vary depending on the amount, type of drug, circumstances, and jurisdiction. A person has possession of drugs if he or she has actual physical control of the drugs (they have the drugs in their hands) or if the drugs are on that person.
Introduction	In an essay, article, or book, an introduction (also known as a prolegomenon) is a beginning section which states the purpose and goals of the following writing. This is generally followed by the body and conclusion.
	The introduction typically describes the scope of the document and gives the brief explanation or summary of the document.
Popularity	Popularity is the quality of being well-liked or common, or having a high social status. Popularity figures are an important part of many people's personal value systems and form a vital component of success in people-oriented fields such as management, politics, and entertainment, among others.
	Borrowed from the Latin popularis in 1490, originally meant 'common' or 'being well-liked'.
Controlled Substances Act	The Controlled Substances Act was enacted into law by the Congress of the United States as Title II of the Comprehensive Drug Abuse Prevention and Control Act of 1970. The CSA is the federal U.S. drug policy under which the manufacture, importation, possession, use and distribution of certain substances is regulated. The Act also served as the national implementing legislation for the Single Convention on Narcotic Drugs.
	The legislation created five Schedules (classifications), with varying qualifications for a substance to be included in each.

3. Drug Policy

Drug prohibition law	Drug prohibition law is prohibition-based law by which governments prohibit, except under licence, the production, supply, and possession of many, but not all, substances which are recognised as drugs, and which corresponds to international treaty commitments in the Single Convention on Narcotic Drugs 1961, the Convention on Psychotropic Substances 1971, and the United Nations Convention Against Illicit Traffic in Narcotic Drugs and Psychotropic Substances 1988.
	When produced, supplied or possessed under licence, otherwise prohibited drugs are known as controlled drugs. The aforementioned legislation is the cultural institution and social fact that de facto divides world drug trade as illegal vs legal, according to geopolitical issues.
Categories	On May 14, 1867, the 27-year-old Charles Sanders Peirce, who eventually founded Pragmatism, presented a paper entitled 'On a New List of Categories' to the American Academy of Arts and Sciences. Among other things, this paper outlined a theory of predication involving three universal categories that Peirce continued to apply in philosophy and elsewhere for the rest of his life. In the categories one will discern, concentrated, the pattern which one finds formed by the three grades of clearness in 'How to Make Our Ideas Clear' (1878 foundational paper for pragmatism), and in numerous other three-way distinctions in his work.
Alcohol dependence	Alcohol dependence is a psychiatric diagnosis (a substance related disorder DSM-IV) describing an entity in which an individual uses alcohol despite significant areas of dysfunction, evidence of physical dependence, and/or related hardship, and also may cause stress and bipolar disorder.
	According to the DSM-IV criteria for alcohol dependence, at least three out of seven of the following criteria must be manifest during a 12 month period:•Tolerance•Withdrawal symptoms or clinically defined Alcohol Withdrawal Syndrome•Use in larger amounts or for longer periods than intended•Persistent desire or unsuccessful efforts to cut down on alcohol use•Time is spent obtaining alcohol or recovering from effects•Social, occupational and recreational pursuits are given up or reduced because of alcohol use•Use is continued despite knowledge of alcohol-related harm (physical or psychological)History and epidemiology
	About 12% of American adults have had an alcohol dependence problem at some time in their life. The term 'alcohol dependence' has replaced 'alcoholism' as a term in order that individuals do not internalize the idea of cure and disease, but can approach alcohol as a chemical they may depend upon to cope with outside pressures.
Uniform Controlled Substances Act	The Uniform Controlled Substances Act was drafted by the United States Department of Justice in 1969 and promulgated by the National Conference of Commissioners on Uniform State Laws while the federal Controlled Substances Act was being drafted. Modeled after the federal Act, the uniform act established a drug scheduling system. Every state has adopted the uniform act.
Screening	Screening in economics refers to a strategy of combating adverse selection, one of the potential decision-making complications in cases of asymmetric information.

3. Drug Policy

	The concept of screening was first developed by Michael Spence (1973), and should be distinguished from signalling, which implies that the informed agent moves first. For purposes of screening, asymmetric information cases assume two economic agents--which we call, for example, Abel and Cain--where Abel knows more about himself than Cain knows about Abel.
Hypothetico-deductive model	The hypothetico-deductive model, first so-named by William Whewell, is a proposed description of scientific method. According to it, scientific inquiry proceeds by formulating a hypothesis in a form that could conceivably be falsified by a test on observable data. A test that could and does run contrary to predictions of the hypothesis is taken as a falsification of the hypothesis.
Border guard	The border guard of a country is a national security agency that performs border control, i.e., enforces the security of the country's national borders. During peacetime special border patrolling forces, the Border guard, mans the chain of Border Outposts which are maintained all along international borders by countries to check smuggling, infiltration by spies of untrusted neighboring countries, insurgents bent on smuggling weapons and explosives for terrorist attacks and subversive activities, illegal immigration and human trafficking etc.. Patrols go out regularly from the Border outposts to patrol the international border to check illegal crossings and track any footprints of those who may have crossed over illegally or attempted to.
Customs	Customs is an authority or agency in a country responsible for collecting and safeguarding customs duties and for controlling the flow of goods including animals, transports, personal effects and hazardous items in and out of a country. Depending on local legislation and regulations, the import or export of some goods may be restricted or forbidden, and the customs agency enforces these rules. The customs authority may be different from the immigration authority, which monitors persons who leave or enter the country, checking for appropriate documentation, apprehending people wanted by international arrest warrants, and impeding the entry of others deemed dangerous to the country.
National park	A national park is a reserve of natural or semi-natural land, declared or owned by a government, set aside for human recreation and enjoyment, animal and environmental protection and restricted from most development. While ideas for national parks had been suggested previously, the first one established, in 1872, was the United States' Yellowstone National Park. An international organization, the International Union for Conservation of Nature (IUCN), and its World Commission on Protected Areas, has defined National Parks as its category II type of protected areas.
Ronald Reagan	Ronald Wilson Reagan (; February 6, 1911 - June 5, 2004) was the 40th President of the United States, serving from 1981 to 1989. Prior to that, he was the 33rd Governor of California from 1967 to 1975 and a radio, film and television actor.

3. Drug Policy

Born in Tampico, Illinois and raised in Dixon, Reagan was educated at Eureka College, earning a Bachelor of Arts degree in economics and sociology. After his graduation, Reagan moved first to Iowa to work as a radio broadcaster and then in to Los Angeles, California in 1937 where he began a career as an actor, first in films and later television. Some of his most notable films include Knute Rockne, All American, Kings Row, and Bedtime for Bonzo. Reagan served as president of the Screen Actors Guild, and later as a spokesman for General Electric (GE); his start in politics occurred during his work for GE. Originally a member of the Democratic Party, his positions began shifting rightward in the late 1950s, and he switched to the Republican Party in 1962. After delivering a rousing speech in support of Barry Goldwater's presidential candidacy in 1964, he was persuaded to seek the California governorship, winning two years later and again in 1970. He was defeated in his run for the Republican presidential nomination in 1968 as well as 1976, but won both the nomination and election in 1980, defeating incumbent Jimmy Carter.

As president, Reagan implemented sweeping new political and economic initiatives. His supply-side economic policies, dubbed 'Reaganomics', advocated reducing tax rates to spur economic growth, controlling the money supply to reduce inflation, deregulation of the economy, and reducing government spending. In his first term he survived an assassination attempt, took a hard line against labor unions, and ordered an invasion of Grenada. He was reelected in a landslide in 1984, proclaiming that it was 'Morning in America.' His second term was primarily marked by foreign matters, such as the ending of the Cold War, the 1986 bombing of Libya, and the revelation of the Iran-Contra affair. Publicly describing the Soviet Union as an 'evil empire,' he supported anti-communist movements worldwide and spent his first term forgoing the strategy of détente by ordering a massive military buildup in an arms race with the USSR. Reagan negotiated with Soviet General Secretary Mikhail Gorbachev, culminating in the INF Treaty and the decrease of both countries' nuclear arsenals.

Reagan left office in 1989. In 1994, the former president disclosed that he had been diagnosed with Alzheimer's disease earlier in the year; he died ten years later at the age of 93. He ranks highly in public opinion polls of U.S. Presidents and is credited for generating an ideological renaissance on the American political right. Early life

Ronald Wilson Reagan was born in an apartment on the second floor of a commercial building in Tampico, Illinois on February 6, 1911, to Jack Reagan and Nelle Wilson Reagan. Reagan's father was a salesman and a storyteller, the grandson of Irish Catholic immigrants from County Tipperary while his mother had Scots and English ancestors. Reagan had one sibling, his older brother, Neil (1908-1996), who became an advertising executive. As a boy, Reagan's father nicknamed his son 'Dutch', due to his 'fat little Dutchman'-like appearance, and his 'Dutchboy' haircut; the nickname stuck with him throughout his youth. Reagan's family briefly lived in several towns and cities in Illinois, including Monmouth, Galesburg and Chicago, until 1919, when they returned to Tampico and lived above the H.C. Pitney Variety Store.

After his election as president, residing in the upstairs White House private quarters, Reagan would quip that he was 'living above the store again'.

According to Paul Kengor, author of God and Ronald Reagan, Reagan had a particularly strong faith in the goodness of people, which stemmed from the optimistic faith of his mother, Nelle, and the Disciples of Christ faith, which he was baptized into in 1922. For the time, Reagan was unusual in his opposition to racial discrimination, and recalled a time in Dixon when the local inn would not allow black people to stay there.

Costs	Costs is a term of art in civil litigation in English law (the law of England and Wales), and in other Commonwealth jurisdictions. After judgment has been given, the judge has the power to order who will pay the lawyers' fees and other disbursements of the parties (the costs). The law of costs defines how such allocation is to take place.
Drug education	Drug education is the planned provision of information and skills relevant to living in a world where drugs are commonly misused. Planning includes developing strategies for helping children and young people engage with relevant drug-related issues during opportunistic and brief contacts with them as well as during more structured sessions. Drug education enables children and young adults to develop the knowledge, skills and attitudes to appreciate the benefits of a healthy lifestyle, promote responsibility towards the use of drugs and relate these to their own actions and those of others, both now and in their future lives.
Consciousness	Consciousness is the quality or state of being aware of an external object or something within oneself. It has been defined as: subjectivity, awareness, sentience, the ability to experience or to feel, wakefulness, having a sense of selfhood, and the executive control system of the mind. Despite the difficulty in definition, many philosophers believe that there is a broadly shared underlying intuition about what consciousness is.

3. Drug Policy

1. The _____, first so-named by William Whewell, is a proposed description of scientific method. According to it, scientific inquiry proceeds by formulating a hypothesis in a form that could conceivably be falsified by a test on observable data. A test that could and does run contrary to predictions of the hypothesis is taken as a falsification of the hypothesis.

   a. Lakatos Award
   b. Hypothetico-deductive model
   c. Medawar Lecture
   d. Mediocrity principle

2. _____, in criminology, is 'the process by which behaviors and individuals are transformed into crime and criminals'. Previously legal acts may be transformed into crimes by legislation or judicial decision. However, there is usually a formal presumption in the rules of statutory interpretation against the retrospective application of laws and only the use of express words by the legislature may rebut this presumption.

   a. Criminalization
   b. Critical criminology
   c. CSI effect
   d. Cui bono

3. _____ is the belief that gradual changes through and within existing institutions of a society can ultimately change a society's fundamental economic relations, economic system, and political structures. This belief grew out of opposition to revolutionary socialism, which contends that revolutions are necessary for fundamental structural changes to occur.

   Socialist _____, or evolutionary socialism, was first put forward by Eduard Bernstein, a leading social democrat.

   a. Religious socialism
   b. Reformism
   c. Ricardian socialism
   d. Right-wing socialism

4. The _____ was enacted into law by the Congress of the United States as Title II of the Comprehensive Drug Abuse Prevention and Control Act of 1970. The CSA is the federal U.S. drug policy under which the manufacture, importation, possession, use and distribution of certain substances is regulated. The Act also served as the national implementing legislation for the Single Convention on Narcotic Drugs.

   The legislation created five Schedules (classifications), with varying qualifications for a substance to be included in each.

   a. Crack epidemic
   b. Drug Abuse Resistance Education
   c. Controlled Substances Act
   d. Just Say No

5. . _____ is the exchange of capital, goods, and services across international borders or territories.

In most countries, such trade represents a significant share of gross domestic product (GDP). While _____ has been present throughout much of history, its economic, social, and political importance has been on the rise in recent centuries.

a. Investment policy
b. ISO 4217
c. International trade
d. Oil boom

1. b
2. a
3. b
4. c
5. c

You can take the complete Chapter Practice Test

for 3. Drug Policy
on all key terms, persons, places, and concepts.

Online 99 Cents

http://www.epub4.1.22005.3.cram101.com/

Use www.Cram101.com for all your study needs

including Cram101's online interactive problem solving labs in

chemistry, statistics, mathematics, and more.

CHAPTER OUTLINE: KEY TERMS, PEOPLE, PLACES, CONCEPTS

	Cocaine
	Homeostasis
	Psychoactive drug
	Axon terminal
	Mental disorder
	Ronald Reagan
	Relocation
	Criminalization
	Substance abuse
	Controlled substance
	Schizophrenia
	Alzheimer's disease
	Mickey Finn
	Dopamine
	Production
	Autonomous language
	Alcohol dependence
	Dopamine transporter
	Mechanism
	Representation
	Schematic

	Intervention
	Monitoring
	Depression
	Monoamine neurotransmitter
	Categories
	Frontal lobe

CHAPTER HIGHLIGHTS & NOTES: KEY TERMS, PEOPLE, PLACES, CONCEPTS

Cocaine	Cocaine is a 1922 British crime film directed by Graham Cutts and starring Hilda Bayley, Flora Le Breton, Ward McAllister and Cyril Raymond. A melodrama - it depicts the distribution of cocaine by gangsters through a series of London nightclubs and the revenge sought by a man after the death of his daughter.
	Because of its depiction of drug use, it was the most controversial British film of the 1920s.
Homeostasis	Homeostasis is the property of a system that regulates its internal environment and tends to maintain a stable, relatively constant condition of properties such as temperature or pH. It can be either an open or closed system. In simple terms, it is a process in which the body's internal environment is kept stable. It was defined by Claude Bernard and later by Walter Bradford Cannon in 1926, 1929 and 1932.
Psychoactive drug	A psychoactive drug, psychopharmaceutical, or psychotropic is a chemical substance that crosses the blood-brain barrier and acts primarily upon the central nervous system where it affects brain function, resulting in changes in perception, mood, consciousness, cognition, and behavior. These substances may be used recreationally, to purposefully alter one's consciousness, as entheogens, for ritual, spiritual, and/or shamanic purposes, as a tool for studying or augmenting the mind, or therapeutically as medication.
	Because psychoactive substances bring about subjective changes in consciousness and mood that the user may find pleasant (e.g. euphoria) or advantageous (e.g.

| Axon terminal | Axon terminals are distal terminations of the branches of an axon. An axon nerve fiber is a long, slender projection of a nerve cell, or neuron, that conducts electrical impulses (called 'action potentials') away from the neuron's cell body, or soma, in order to transmit those impulses to other neurons.

Neurons are interconnected in complex arrangements, and use electrochemical signals and neurotransmitter chemicals to transmit impulses from one neuron to the next; axon terminals are separated from neighboring neurons by a small gap called a synapse, across which impulses are sent. |
| --- | --- |
| Mental disorder | A mental disorder or mental illness is a psychological pattern or anomaly, potentially reflected in behavior, that is generally associated with distress or disability, and which is not considered part of normal development of a person's culture. Mental disorders are generally defined by a combination of how a person feels, acts, thinks or perceives. This may be associated with particular regions or functions of the brain or rest of the nervous system, often in a social context. |
| Ronald Reagan | Ronald Wilson Reagan (; February 6, 1911 - June 5, 2004) was the 40th President of the United States, serving from 1981 to 1989. Prior to that, he was the 33rd Governor of California from 1967 to 1975 and a radio, film and television actor.

Born in Tampico, Illinois and raised in Dixon, Reagan was educated at Eureka College, earning a Bachelor of Arts degree in economics and sociology. After his graduation, Reagan moved first to Iowa to work as a radio broadcaster and then in to Los Angeles, California in 1937 where he began a career as an actor, first in films and later television. Some of his most notable films include Knute Rockne, All American, Kings Row, and Bedtime for Bonzo. Reagan served as president of the Screen Actors Guild, and later as a spokesman for General Electric (GE); his start in politics occurred during his work for GE. Originally a member of the Democratic Party, his positions began shifting rightward in the late 1950s, and he switched to the Republican Party in 1962. After delivering a rousing speech in support of Barry Goldwater's presidential candidacy in 1964, he was persuaded to seek the California governorship, winning two years later and again in 1970. He was defeated in his run for the Republican presidential nomination in 1968 as well as 1976, but won both the nomination and election in 1980, defeating incumbent Jimmy Carter.

As president, Reagan implemented sweeping new political and economic initiatives. His supply-side economic policies, dubbed 'Reaganomics', advocated reducing tax rates to spur economic growth, controlling the money supply to reduce inflation, deregulation of the economy, and reducing government spending. In his first term he survived an assassination attempt, took a hard line against labor unions, and ordered an invasion of Grenada. He was reelected in a landslide in 1984, proclaiming that it was 'Morning in America.' His second term was primarily marked by foreign matters, such as the ending of the Cold War, the 1986 bombing of Libya, and the revelation of the Iran-Contra affair. |

4. The Nervous System

Publicly describing the Soviet Union as an 'evil empire,' he supported anti-communist movements worldwide and spent his first term forgoing the strategy of détente by ordering a massive military buildup in an arms race with the USSR. Reagan negotiated with Soviet General Secretary Mikhail Gorbachev, culminating in the INF Treaty and the decrease of both countries' nuclear arsenals.

Reagan left office in 1989. In 1994, the former president disclosed that he had been diagnosed with Alzheimer's disease earlier in the year; he died ten years later at the age of 93. He ranks highly in public opinion polls of U.S. Presidents and is credited for generating an ideological renaissance on the American political right. Early life

Ronald Wilson Reagan was born in an apartment on the second floor of a commercial building in Tampico, Illinois on February 6, 1911, to Jack Reagan and Nelle Wilson Reagan. Reagan's father was a salesman and a storyteller, the grandson of Irish Catholic immigrants from County Tipperary while his mother had Scots and English ancestors. Reagan had one sibling, his older brother, Neil (1908-1996), who became an advertising executive. As a boy, Reagan's father nicknamed his son 'Dutch', due to his 'fat little Dutchman'-like appearance, and his 'Dutchboy' haircut; the nickname stuck with him throughout his youth. Reagan's family briefly lived in several towns and cities in Illinois, including Monmouth, Galesburg and Chicago, until 1919, when they returned to Tampico and lived above the H.C. Pitney Variety Store. After his election as president, residing in the upstairs White House private quarters, Reagan would quip that he was 'living above the store again'.

According to Paul Kengor, author of God and Ronald Reagan, Reagan had a particularly strong faith in the goodness of people, which stemmed from the optimistic faith of his mother, Nelle, and the Disciples of Christ faith, which he was baptized into in 1922. For the time, Reagan was unusual in his opposition to racial discrimination, and recalled a time in Dixon when the local inn would not allow black people to stay there.

Relocation	Relocation is the process of vacating a fixed location (such as a residence or business) and settling in a different one. A move can be to a nearby location within the same neighborhood, a much farther location in a different city, or sometimes a different country. On the Holmes and Rahe stress scale for adults, 'change of residence' is considered a stressful activity, assigned 20 points (with death of spouse being ranked the highest at 100), although other changes on the scale (e.g. 'change in living conditions', 'change in social activities') often occur as a result of relocating, making the overall stress level potentially higher.
Criminalization	Criminalization, in criminology, is 'the process by which behaviors and individuals are transformed into crime and criminals'. Previously legal acts may be transformed into crimes by legislation or judicial decision. However, there is usually a formal presumption in the rules of statutory interpretation against the retrospective application of laws and only the use of express words by the legislature may rebut this presumption.

4. The Nervous System

Substance abuse	Substance abuse, also known as drug abuse, is a patterned use of a substance (drug) in which the user consumes the substance in amounts or with methods neither approved nor supervised by medical professionals. Substance abuse/drug abuse is not limited to mood-altering or psycho-active drugs. If an activity is performed using the objects against the rules and policies of the matter (as in steroids for performance enhancement in sports), it is also called substance abuse.
Controlled substance	A controlled substance is generally a drug or chemical whose manufacture, possession, and use are regulated by a government. This may include illegal drugs and prescription medications (designated Controlled Drug in the United Kingdom).
Schizophrenia	Schizophrenia is a mental disorder characterized by a breakdown of thought processes and by poor emotional responsiveness. Common symptoms include auditory hallucinations, paranoid or bizarre delusions, or disorganized speech and thinking, and it is accompanied by significant social or occupational dysfunction. The onset of symptoms typically occurs in young adulthood, with a global lifetime prevalence of about 0.3-0.7%.
Alzheimer's disease	Alzheimer's disease also known in medical literature as Alzheimer disease, is the most common form of dementia. There is no cure for the disease, which worsens as it progresses, and eventually leads to death. Most often, Alzheimer's disease is diagnosed in people over 65 years of age, although the less-prevalent early-onset Alzheimer's disease can occur much earlier. In 2006, there were 26.6 million sufferers worldwide.
Mickey Finn	A Mickey Finn is a slang term for a drink laced with a drug (especially chloral hydrate) given to someone without their knowledge in order to incapacitate them. Serving someone a Mickey Finn is most commonly referred to as slipping a mickey, sometimes spelled 'slipping a mickie'. History of term The Chicago bartender Michael 'Mickey' Finn The Mickey Finn is most likely named for the manager and bartender of a Chicago establishment, the Lone Star Saloon and Palm Garden Restaurant, which operated from 1896 to 1903 in the city's South Loop neighborhood on South State Street.
Dopamine	Dopamine is a catecholamine neurotransmitter present in a wide variety of animals, including both vertebrates and invertebrates. In the brain, this substituted phenethylamine functions as a neurotransmitter, activating the five known types of dopamine receptors--D_1, D_2, D_3, D_4, and D_5--and their variants. Dopamine is produced in several areas of the brain, including the substantia nigra and the ventral tegmental area.
Production	In economics, production is the act of creating output, a good or service which has value and contributes to the utility of individuals.

4. The Nervous System

The act may or may not include factors of production other than labor. Any effort directed toward the realization of a desired product or service is a 'productive' effort and the performance of such act is production.

Autonomous language	An autonomous language is usually a standard language that has its own established norms, as opposed to a heteronomous variety.
	An autonomous language will usually have grammar books, dictionaries and literature written in it. Autonomy is largely a sociopolitical construct rather than a result of specific linguistic differences.
Alcohol dependence	Alcohol dependence is a psychiatric diagnosis (a substance related disorder DSM-IV) describing an entity in which an individual uses alcohol despite significant areas of dysfunction, evidence of physical dependence, and/or related hardship, and also may cause stress and bipolar disorder.
	According to the DSM-IV criteria for alcohol dependence, at least three out of seven of the following criteria must be manifest during a 12 month period:•Tolerance•Withdrawal symptoms or clinically defined Alcohol Withdrawal Syndrome•Use in larger amounts or for longer periods than intended•Persistent desire or unsuccessful efforts to cut down on alcohol use•Time is spent obtaining alcohol or recovering from effects•Social, occupational and recreational pursuits are given up or reduced because of alcohol use•Use is continued despite knowledge of alcohol-related harm (physical or psychological)History and epidemiology
	About 12% of American adults have had an alcohol dependence problem at some time in their life. The term 'alcohol dependence' has replaced 'alcoholism' as a term in order that individuals do not internalize the idea of cure and disease, but can approach alcohol as a chemical they may depend upon to cope with outside pressures.
Dopamine transporter	The dopamine transporter is a membrane-spanning protein that pumps the neurotransmitter dopamine out of the synapse back into cytosol, from which other transporters sequester DA and NE into vesicles for later storage and release. Dopamine reuptake via DAT provides the primary mechanism through which dopamine is cleared from synapses except in the prefrontal cortex, where dopamine uptake via the norepinephrine transporter plays that role.
	DAT is thought to be implicated in a number of dopamine-related disorders, including attention deficit hyperactivity disorder, bipolar disorder, clinical depression, and alcoholism.
Mechanism	The term Social mechanisms and mechanism-based explanations of social phenomenon originate from the philosophy of science.
	The core idea behind the mechanism approach has been expressed as follows by Elster (1989: 3-4): 'To explain an event is to give an account of why it happened.

Representation	Representation is the use of signs that stand in for and take the place of something else. It is through representation that people organize the world and reality through the act of naming its elements. Signs are arranged in order to form semantic constructions and express relations.
Schematic	A schematic diagram represents the elements of a system using abstract, graphic symbols rather than realistic pictures. A schematic usually omits all details that are not relevant to the information the schematic is intended to convey, and may add unrealistic elements that aid comprehension. For example, a subway map intended for riders may represent a subway station with a dot; the dot doesn't resemble the actual station at all but gives the viewer information without unnecessary visual clutter.
Intervention	In law, intervention is a procedure to allow a nonparty, called intervenor (also spelled intervener) to join ongoing litigation, either as a matter of right or at the discretion of the court, without the permission of the original litigants. The basic rationale for intervention is that a judgment in a particular case may affect the rights of nonparties, who ideally should have the right to be heard.

Intervenors are most common in appellate proceedings, but can also appear at other types of legal proceeding such as a trial. |
| Monitoring | In medicine, monitoring is the evaluation of a disease or condition over time.

It can be performed by continuously measuring certain parameters (for example, by continuously measuring vital signs by a bedside monitor), and/or by repeatedly performing medical tests (such as blood glucose monitoring in people with diabetes mellitus).

Transmitting data from a monitor to a distant monitoring station is known as telemetry or biotelemetry. |
| Depression | In economics, a depression is a sustained, long-term downturn in economic activity in one or more economies. It is a more severe downturn than a recession, which is seen by some economists as part of the modern business cycle.

Considered by some economists to be a rare and extreme form of recession, a depression is characterized by its length; by abnormally large increases in unemployment; falls in the availability of credit, often due to some kind of banking or financial crisis; shrinking output as buyers dry up and suppliers cut back on production and investment; large number of bankruptcies including sovereign debt defaults; significantly reduced amounts of trade and commerce, especially international; as well as highly volatile relative currency value fluctuations, most often due to devaluations. |
| Monoamine neurotransmitter | Monoamine neurotransmitters are neurotransmitters and neuromodulators that contain one amino group that is connected to an aromatic ring by a two-carbon chain ($-CH_2-CH_2-$). |

4. The Nervous System

Categories	On May 14, 1867, the 27-year-old Charles Sanders Peirce, who eventually founded Pragmatism, presented a paper entitled 'On a New List of Categories' to the American Academy of Arts and Sciences. Among other things, this paper outlined a theory of predication involving three universal categories that Peirce continued to apply in philosophy and elsewhere for the rest of his life. In the categories one will discern, concentrated, the pattern which one finds formed by the three grades of clearness in 'How to Make Our Ideas Clear' (1878 foundational paper for pragmatism), and in numerous other three-way distinctions in his work.
Frontal lobe	The frontal lobe is an area in the brain of humans and other mammals, located at the front of each cerebral hemisphere and positioned anterior to (in front of) the parietal lobe and superior and anterior to the temporal lobes. It is separated from the parietal lobe by a space between tissues called the central sulcus, and from the temporal lobe by a deep fold called the lateral (Sylvian) sulcus. The post-central gyrus, forming the posterior border of the frontal lobe, contains the primary motor cortex, which controls voluntary movements of specific body parts.

1. _____ is a 1922 British crime film directed by Graham Cutts and starring Hilda Bayley, Flora Le Breton, Ward McAllister and Cyril Raymond. A melodrama - it depicts the distribution of _____ by gangsters through a series of London nightclubs and the revenge sought by a man after the death of his daughter.

   Because of its depiction of drug use, it was the most controversial British film of the 1920s.

   a. Deadlock
   b. Cocaine
   c. The Flying Scot
   d. Gangs of New York

2. _____ also known in medical literature as Alzheimer disease, is the most common form of dementia. There is no cure for the disease, which worsens as it progresses, and eventually leads to death. Most often, _____ is diagnosed in people over 65 years of age, although the less-prevalent early-onset _____ can occur much earlier. In 2006, there were 26.6 million sufferers worldwide.

   a. Alzheimer's disease
   b. Developmental disability
   c. Generalized anxiety disorder
   d. bulimia

3. _____ is a catecholamine neurotransmitter present in a wide variety of animals, including both vertebrates and invertebrates. In the brain, this substituted phenethylamine functions as a neurotransmitter, activating the five known types of _____ receptors--D_1, D_2, D_3, D_4, and D_5--and their variants. _____ is produced in several areas of the brain, including the substantia nigra and the ventral tegmental area.

   a. Dopamine
   b. FISH! philosophy
   c. Generalized expected utility
   d. Goal orientation

4. On May 14, 1867, the 27-year-old Charles Sanders Peirce, who eventually founded Pragmatism, presented a paper entitled 'On a New List of _____' to the American Academy of Arts and Sciences. Among other things, this paper outlined a theory of predication involving three universal _____ that Peirce continued to apply in philosophy and elsewhere for the rest of his life. In the _____ one will discern, concentrated, the pattern which one finds formed by the three grades of clearness in 'How to Make Our Ideas Clear' (1878 foundational paper for pragmatism), and in numerous other three-way distinctions in his work.

   a. Categories
   b. Configurational analysis
   c. Counter-experience
   d. Jacques Derrida

5. _____ is the property of a system that regulates its internal environment and tends to maintain a stable, relatively constant condition of properties such as temperature or pH. It can be either an open or closed system. In simple terms, it is a process in which the body's internal environment is kept stable. It was defined by Claude Bernard and later by Walter Bradford Cannon in 1926, 1929 and 1932.

   a. Visa overstay
   b. The Embezzler
   c. The Flying Scot
   d. Homeostasis

1. b
2. a
3. a
4. a
5. d

You can take the complete Chapter Practice Test

for 4. The Nervous System
on all key terms, persons, places, and concepts.

Online 99 Cents

http://www.epub4.1.22005.4.cram101.com/

Use www.Cram101.com for all your study needs

including Cram101's online interactive problem solving labs in

chemistry, statistics, mathematics, and more.

5. The Actions of Drugs

_____ | Categories

_____ | Chemical imbalance

_____ | Direct evidence

_____ | Rating scale

_____ | Amotivational syndrome

_____ | Aripiprazole

_____ | Mechanism

_____ | Narcotic

_____ | Prescription

_____ | Bad trip

_____ | Dose-response relationship

_____ | Lethal injection

_____ | Cocaine

_____ | Substance abuse

_____ | Psychoactive drug

_____ | Agent

_____ | Drug education

_____ | Seriousness

_____ | Administration

_____ | Criminalization

_____ | Benjamin Rush

5. The Actions of Drugs

	Alcohol dependence
	Absorption
	Skin popping
	Distribution
	Ronald Reagan
	Relocation
	Refusal skills
	Slow Down
	Discovery
	Induction
	Physical dependence

Categories — On May 14, 1867, the 27-year-old Charles Sanders Peirce, who eventually founded Pragmatism, presented a paper entitled 'On a New List of Categories' to the American Academy of Arts and Sciences. Among other things, this paper outlined a theory of predication involving three universal categories that Peirce continued to apply in philosophy and elsewhere for the rest of his life. In the categories one will discern, concentrated, the pattern which one finds formed by the three grades of clearness in 'How to Make Our Ideas Clear' (1878 foundational paper for pragmatism), and in numerous other three-way distinctions in his work.

Chemical imbalance — Chemical imbalance is one hypothesis about the cause of mental illness. Other causes that are debated include psychological and social causes.

5. The Actions of Drugs

Direct evidence	Direct evidence supports the truth of an assertion (in criminal law, an assertion of guilt or of innocence) directly, i.e., without an intervening inference. Circumstantial evidence, by contrast, consists of a fact or set of facts which, if proven, will support the creation of an inference that the matter asserted is true. For example: a witness who testifies that he saw the defendant shoot the victim gives direct evidence.
Rating scale	A rating scale is a set of categories designed to elicit information about a quantitative or a qualitative attribute. In the social sciences, common examples are the Likert scale and 1-10 rating scales in which a person selects the number which is considered to reflect the perceived quality of a product. A rating scale is a method that requires the rater to assign a value, sometimes numeric, to the rated object, as a measure of some rated attribute.
Amotivational syndrome	Amotivational syndrome is a psychological condition associated with diminished inspiration to participate in social situations and activities, with lapses in apathy caused by an external event, situation, substance , relationship , or other cause. While some have claimed that chronic use of cannabis causes amotivational syndrome in some users, empirical studies suggest that there is no such thing as 'amotivational syndrome', per se. From a World Health Organization report: A study done by researchers Barnwell, Earleywine and Wilcox on a sample of undergraduates also suggests that cannabis use does not cause an amotivational syndrome.
Aripiprazole	Aripiprazole is an atypical antipsychotic and antidepressant used in the treatment of schizophrenia, bipolar disorder, and clinical depression. It was approved by the US Food and Drug Administration (FDA) for schizophrenia on November 15, 2002 and the European Medicines Agency on 4th of June 2004; for acute manic and mixed episodes associated with bipolar disorder on October 1, 2004; as an adjunct for major depressive disorder on November 20, 2007; and to treat irritability in children with autism on 20 November 2009. Aripiprazole was developed by Otsuka in Japan, and in the United States, Otsuka America markets it jointly with Bristol-Myers Squibb. Aripiprazole is used for the treatment of schizophrenia or bipolar disorder.
Mechanism	The term Social mechanisms and mechanism-based explanations of social phenomenon originate from the philosophy of science. The core idea behind the mechanism approach has been expressed as follows by Elster (1989: 3-4): 'To explain an event is to give an account of why it happened.

Narcotic	The term narcotic originally referred medically to any psychoactive compound with sleep-inducing properties. In the United States of America it has since become associated with opioids, commonly morphine and heroin. The term is, today, imprecisely defined and typically has negative connotations.
Prescription	In law, prescription is the method of sovereignty transfer of a territory through international law analogous to the common law doctrine of adverse possession for private real-estate. Prescription involves the open encroachment by the new sovereign upon the territory in question for a prolonged period of time, acting as the sovereign, without protest or other contest by the original sovereign. This doctrine legalizes de jure the de facto transfer of sovereignty caused in part by the original sovereign's extended negligence and/or neglect of the area in question.
Bad trip	Bad trip is a disturbing experience sometimes associated with use of a psychedelic drug such as LSD, Salvinorin A, DXM, mescaline, psilocybin, DMT and sometimes even other drugs including alcohol and MDMA. The manifestations can range from feelings of vague anxiety and alienation to profoundly disturbing states of unrelieved terror, ultimate entrapment, or cosmic annihilation. Psychedelic specialists in the therapeutic community do not necessarily consider unpleasant experiences as threatening or negative, focusing instead on their potential to be highly beneficial to the user when properly resolved. They can be exacerbated by the inexperience or irresponsibility of the user or the lack of proper preparation and environment for the trip, and are reflective of unresolved psychological tensions triggered during the course of the experience.
Dose-response relationship	The dose-response relationship, describes the change in effect on an organism caused by differing levels of exposure (or doses) to a stressor (usually a chemical) after a certain exposure time . This may apply to individuals (e.g.: a small amount has no significant effect, a large amount is fatal), or to populations (e.g.: how many people or organisms are affected at different levels of exposure). Studying dose response, and developing dose response models, is central to determining 'safe' and 'hazardous' levels and dosages for drugs, potential pollutants, and other substances to which humans or other organisms are exposed.
Lethal injection	Lethal injection is the practice of injecting a person with a fatal dose of drugs (typically a barbiturate, paralytic, and potassium solution) for the express purpose of causing the immediate death of the subject. The main application for this procedure is capital punishment, but the term may also be applied in a broad sense to euthanasia and suicide. It kills the person by first putting the person to sleep, then stopping the breathing and heart in that order.
Cocaine	Cocaine is a 1922 British crime film directed by Graham Cutts and starring Hilda Bayley, Flora Le Breton, Ward McAllister and Cyril Raymond. A melodrama - it depicts the distribution of cocaine by gangsters through a series of London nightclubs and the revenge sought by a man after the death of his daughter.

5. The Actions of Drugs

Substance abuse	Substance abuse, also known as drug abuse, is a patterned use of a substance (drug) in which the user consumes the substance in amounts or with methods neither approved nor supervised by medical professionals. Substance abuse/drug abuse is not limited to mood-altering or psycho-active drugs. If an activity is performed using the objects against the rules and policies of the matter (as in steroids for performance enhancement in sports), it is also called substance abuse.
Psychoactive drug	A psychoactive drug, psychopharmaceutical, or psychotropic is a chemical substance that crosses the blood-brain barrier and acts primarily upon the central nervous system where it affects brain function, resulting in changes in perception, mood, consciousness, cognition, and behavior. These substances may be used recreationally, to purposefully alter one's consciousness, as entheogens, for ritual, spiritual, and/or shamanic purposes, as a tool for studying or augmenting the mind, or therapeutically as medication.
	Because psychoactive substances bring about subjective changes in consciousness and mood that the user may find pleasant (e.g. euphoria) or advantageous (e.g. increased alertness), many psychoactive substances are abused, that is, used excessively, despite health risks or negative consequences.
Agent	In economics, an agent is an actor and decision maker in a model. Typically, every agent makes decisions by solving a well or ill defined optimization/choice problem. The term agent can also be seen as equivalent to player in game theory.
Drug education	Drug education is the planned provision of information and skills relevant to living in a world where drugs are commonly misused. Planning includes developing strategies for helping children and young people engage with relevant drug-related issues during opportunistic and brief contacts with them as well as during more structured sessions. Drug education enables children and young adults to develop the knowledge, skills and attitudes to appreciate the benefits of a healthy lifestyle, promote responsibility towards the use of drugs and relate these to their own actions and those of others, both now and in their future lives.
Seriousness	Seriousness is an attiude of gravity, solemnity, persistence, and earnestness toward something considered to be of importance.
	Some notable philosophers and commentators have criticised excessive seriousness, while others have praised it. Seriousness is often contrasted with comedy, as in the seriocomedy.
Administration	As a legal concept, administration is a procedure under the insolvency laws of a number of common law jurisdictions. It functions as a rescue mechanism for insolvent entities and allows them to carry on running their business. The process - an alternative to liquidation - is often known as going into administration.

5. The Actions of Drugs

Criminalization	Criminalization, in criminology, is 'the process by which behaviors and individuals are transformed into crime and criminals'. Previously legal acts may be transformed into crimes by legislation or judicial decision. However, there is usually a formal presumption in the rules of statutory interpretation against the retrospective application of laws and only the use of express words by the legislature may rebut this presumption.
Benjamin Rush	Benjamin Rush was a Founding Father of the United States. Rush lived in the state of Pennsylvania and was a physician, writer, educator, humanitarian and a Christian Universalist, as well as the founder of Dickinson College in Carlisle, Pennsylvania. Rush was a signatory of the Declaration of Independence and attended the Continental Congress.
Alcohol dependence	Alcohol dependence is a psychiatric diagnosis (a substance related disorder DSM-IV) describing an entity in which an individual uses alcohol despite significant areas of dysfunction, evidence of physical dependence, and/or related hardship, and also may cause stress and bipolar disorder. According to the DSM-IV criteria for alcohol dependence, at least three out of seven of the following criteria must be manifest during a 12 month period:•Tolerance•Withdrawal symptoms or clinically defined Alcohol Withdrawal Syndrome•Use in larger amounts or for longer periods than intended•Persistent desire or unsuccessful efforts to cut down on alcohol use•Time is spent obtaining alcohol or recovering from effects•Social, occupational and recreational pursuits are given up or reduced because of alcohol use•Use is continued despite knowledge of alcohol-related harm (physical or psychological)History and epidemiology About 12% of American adults have had an alcohol dependence problem at some time in their life. The term 'alcohol dependence' has replaced 'alcoholism' as a term in order that individuals do not internalize the idea of cure and disease, but can approach alcohol as a chemical they may depend upon to cope with outside pressures.
Absorption	In economics, absorption is the total demand for all final marketed goods and services by all economic agents resident in an economy, regardless of the origin of the goods and services themselves. As the absorption is equal to the sum of all domestically-produced goods consumed locally and all imports, it is equal to national income [Y = C + I + G + (X - M)] minus the balance of trade [X - M]. The term was coined, and its relation to the balance of trade identified, by Sidney Alexander in 1952.
Skin popping	Skin popping is a method of administration for the use of drugs by injecting or placing the substance or drug under the skin. It can include subcutaneous placement or intradermal placement though is also rarely used to mean intramuscular injection.

5. The Actions of Drugs

Distribution	Distribution in economics refers to the way total output, income, or wealth is distributed among individuals or among the factors of production (such as labour, land, and capital).. In general theory and the national income and product accounts, each unit of output corresponds to a unit of income. One use of national accounts is for classifying factor incomes and measuring their respective shares, as in National Income.
Ronald Reagan	Ronald Wilson Reagan (; February 6, 1911 - June 5, 2004) was the 40th President of the United States, serving from 1981 to 1989. Prior to that, he was the 33rd Governor of California from 1967 to 1975 and a radio, film and television actor.
	Born in Tampico, Illinois and raised in Dixon, Reagan was educated at Eureka College, earning a Bachelor of Arts degree in economics and sociology. After his graduation, Reagan moved first to Iowa to work as a radio broadcaster and then in to Los Angeles, California in 1937 where he began a career as an actor, first in films and later television. Some of his most notable films include Knute Rockne, All American, Kings Row, and Bedtime for Bonzo. Reagan served as president of the Screen Actors Guild, and later as a spokesman for General Electric (GE); his start in politics occurred during his work for GE. Originally a member of the Democratic Party, his positions began shifting rightward in the late 1950s, and he switched to the Republican Party in 1962. After delivering a rousing speech in support of Barry Goldwater's presidential candidacy in 1964, he was persuaded to seek the California governorship, winning two years later and again in 1970. He was defeated in his run for the Republican presidential nomination in 1968 as well as 1976, but won both the nomination and election in 1980, defeating incumbent Jimmy Carter.
	As president, Reagan implemented sweeping new political and economic initiatives. His supply-side economic policies, dubbed 'Reaganomics', advocated reducing tax rates to spur economic growth, controlling the money supply to reduce inflation, deregulation of the economy, and reducing government spending. In his first term he survived an assassination attempt, took a hard line against labor unions, and ordered an invasion of Grenada. He was reelected in a landslide in 1984, proclaiming that it was 'Morning in America.' His second term was primarily marked by foreign matters, such as the ending of the Cold War, the 1986 bombing of Libya, and the revelation of the Iran-Contra affair. Publicly describing the Soviet Union as an 'evil empire,' he supported anti-communist movements worldwide and spent his first term forgoing the strategy of détente by ordering a massive military buildup in an arms race with the USSR. Reagan negotiated with Soviet General Secretary Mikhail Gorbachev, culminating in the INF Treaty and the decrease of both countries' nuclear arsenals.
	Reagan left office in 1989. In 1994, the former president disclosed that he had been diagnosed with Alzheimer's disease earlier in the year; he died ten years later at the age of 93. He ranks highly in public opinion polls of U.S. Presidents and is credited for generating an ideological renaissance on the American political right. Early life

Ronald Wilson Reagan was born in an apartment on the second floor of a commercial building in Tampico, Illinois on February 6, 1911, to Jack Reagan and Nelle Wilson Reagan. Reagan's father was a salesman and a storyteller, the grandson of Irish Catholic immigrants from County Tipperary while his mother had Scots and English ancestors. Reagan had one sibling, his older brother, Neil (1908-1996), who became an advertising executive. As a boy, Reagan's father nicknamed his son 'Dutch', due to his 'fat little Dutchman'-like appearance, and his 'Dutchboy' haircut; the nickname stuck with him throughout his youth. Reagan's family briefly lived in several towns and cities in Illinois, including Monmouth, Galesburg and Chicago, until 1919, when they returned to Tampico and lived above the H.C. Pitney Variety Store. After his election as president, residing in the upstairs White House private quarters, Reagan would quip that he was 'living above the store again'.

According to Paul Kengor, author of God and Ronald Reagan, Reagan had a particularly strong faith in the goodness of people, which stemmed from the optimistic faith of his mother, Nelle, and the Disciples of Christ faith, which he was baptized into in 1922. For the time, Reagan was unusual in his opposition to racial discrimination, and recalled a time in Dixon when the local inn would not allow black people to stay there.

Relocation

Relocation is the process of vacating a fixed location (such as a residence or business) and settling in a different one. A move can be to a nearby location within the same neighborhood, a much farther location in a different city, or sometimes a different country. On the Holmes and Rahe stress scale for adults, 'change of residence' is considered a stressful activity, assigned 20 points (with death of spouse being ranked the highest at 100), although other changes on the scale (e.g. 'change in living conditions', 'change in social activities') often occur as a result of relocating, making the overall stress level potentially higher.

Refusal skills

Refusal skills are a set of skills designed to help children avoid participating in high-risk behaviors. Programs designed to discourage crime, drug use, violence, and/or sexual activity frequently include refusal skills in their curricula to help students resist peer pressure while maintaining self-respect. One such program is Drug Abuse Resistance Education.

Slow Down

Slow Down is a sound recorded on May 19, 1997, in the Equatorial Pacific Ocean by the U.S. National Oceanic and Atmospheric Administration. The source of the sound remains unknown.

Analysis

The name was given because the sound slowly decreases in frequency over about 7 minutes.

Discovery

Discovery is the act of detecting something new, or something 'old' that had been unknown.

5. The Actions of Drugs

	With reference to science and academic disciplines, discovery is the observation of new phenomena, new actions, or new events and providing new reasoning to explain the knowledge gathered through such observations with previously acquired knowledge from abstract thought and everyday experiences. Visual discoveries are often called sightings.
Induction	An Induction in a play is an explanatory scene or other intrusion that stands outside and apart from the main action with the intent to comment on it, moralize about it or in the case of dumb show to summarize the plot or underscore what is afoot. Inductions are a common feature of plays written and performed in the Renaissance period, including those of Shakespeare. Example of inductions in Shakespeare are the dumb show in Hamlet and the address to the audience by Puck in A Midsummer Night's Dream.
Physical dependence	Physical dependence refers to a state resulting from chronic use of a drug that has produced tolerance and where negative physical symptoms of withdrawal result from abrupt discontinuation or dosage reduction. Physical dependence can develop from low-dose therapeutic use of certain medications such as benzodiazepines, opioids, antiepileptics and antidepressants, as well as misuse of recreational drugs such as alcohol, opioids and benzodiazepines. The higher the dose used, the greater the duration of use, and the earlier age use began are predictive of worsened physical dependence and thus more severe withdrawal syndromes.

1. On May 14, 1867, the 27-year-old Charles Sanders Peirce, who eventually founded Pragmatism, presented a paper entitled 'On a New List of _____' to the American Academy of Arts and Sciences. Among other things, this paper outlined a theory of predication involving three universal _____ that Peirce continued to apply in philosophy and elsewhere for the rest of his life. In the _____ one will discern, concentrated, the pattern which one finds formed by the three grades of clearness in 'How to Make Our Ideas Clear' (1878 foundational paper for pragmatism), and in numerous other three-way distinctions in his work.

    a. Central European Institute of Philosophy
    b. Configurational analysis
    c. Counter-experience
    d. Categories

2. . _____ is the practice of injecting a person with a fatal dose of drugs (typically a barbiturate, paralytic, and potassium solution) for the express purpose of causing the immediate death of the subject. The main application for this procedure is capital punishment, but the term may also be applied in a broad sense to euthanasia and suicide. It kills the person by first putting the person to sleep, then stopping the breathing and heart in that order.

a. Marooning
b. Lethal injection
c. Necklacing
d. Nitrogen asphyxiation

3. _____, in criminology, is 'the process by which behaviors and individuals are transformed into crime and criminals'. Previously legal acts may be transformed into crimes by legislation or judicial decision. However, there is usually a formal presumption in the rules of statutory interpretation against the retrospective application of laws and only the use of express words by the legislature may rebut this presumption.

a. Criminaloid
b. Critical criminology
c. Criminalization
d. Cui bono

4. _____ is the process of vacating a fixed location (such as a residence or business) and settling in a different one. A move can be to a nearby location within the same neighborhood, a much farther location in a different city, or sometimes a different country. On the Holmes and Rahe stress scale for adults, 'change of residence' is considered a stressful activity, assigned 20 points (with death of spouse being ranked the highest at 100), although other changes on the scale (e.g. 'change in living conditions', 'change in social activities') often occur as a result of relocating, making the overall stress level potentially higher.

a. Relocation
b. Reverse brain drain
c. Rubanisation
d. Rural flight

5. _____ is a disturbing experience sometimes associated with use of a psychedelic drug such as LSD, Salvinorin A, DXM, mescaline, psilocybin, DMT and sometimes even other drugs including alcohol and MDMA. The manifestations can range from feelings of vague anxiety and alienation to profoundly disturbing states of unrelieved terror, ultimate entrapment, or cosmic annihilation. Psychedelic specialists in the therapeutic community do not necessarily consider unpleasant experiences as threatening or negative, focusing instead on their potential to be highly beneficial to the user when properly resolved. They can be exacerbated by the inexperience or irresponsibility of the user or the lack of proper preparation and environment for the trip, and are reflective of unresolved psychological tensions triggered during the course of the experience.

a. Beatnik
b. The Big Cube
c. Bad trip
d. The Chemical Religion

1. d
2. b
3. c
4. a
5. c

You can take the complete Chapter Practice Test

for 5. The Actions of Drugs
on all key terms, persons, places, and concepts.

Online 99 Cents

http://www.epub4.1.22005.5.cram101.com/

Use www.Cram101.com for all your study needs

including Cram101's online interactive problem solving labs in

chemistry, statistics, mathematics, and more.

6. Stimulants

Cocaine

Sigmund Freud

Crack cocaine

Wealth

Ronald Reagan

Mechanism

Discovery

Drug user

Homeland security

Physical dependence

Monitoring

Smuggling

Adderall

Benzedrine

Amotivational syndrome

Amphetamine

Alcohol dependence

Heroin

Inheritance

Methamphetamine

Dopamine

CHAPTER OUTLINE: KEY TERMS, PEOPLE, PLACES, CONCEPTS

	Monoamine neurotransmitter
	Psilocybin
	Absorption
	Prescription
	Paranoia
	Stimulation

CHAPTER HIGHLIGHTS & NOTES: KEY TERMS, PEOPLE, PLACES, CONCEPTS

Cocaine	Cocaine is a 1922 British crime film directed by Graham Cutts and starring Hilda Bayley, Flora Le Breton, Ward McAllister and Cyril Raymond. A melodrama - it depicts the distribution of cocaine by gangsters through a series of London nightclubs and the revenge sought by a man after the death of his daughter.
	Because of its depiction of drug use, it was the most controversial British film of the 1920s.
Sigmund Freud	Sigmund Freud was an Austrian neurologist who became known as the founding father of psychoanalysis.
	Freud's parents were poor, but they ensured his education. Freud chose medicine as a career and qualified as a doctor at the University of Vienna, subsequently undertaking research into cerebral palsy, aphasia and microscopic neuroanatomy at the Vienna General Hospital.
Crack cocaine	Crack cocaine is the freebase form of cocaine that can be smoked. It may also be termed rock, hard, iron, cavvy, base, or just crack.
	Appearance and characteristics
	In purer forms, crack rocks appear as off-white nuggets with jagged edges, with a slightly higher density than candle wax.

6. Stimulants

Wealth	Wealth is the abundance of valuable resources or material possessions, or the control of such assets. The word wealth is derived from the old English wela, which is from an Indo-European word stem. An individual, community, region or country that possesses an abundance of such possessions or resources is known as wealthy.
Ronald Reagan	Ronald Wilson Reagan (; February 6, 1911 - June 5, 2004) was the 40th President of the United States, serving from 1981 to 1989. Prior to that, he was the 33rd Governor of California from 1967 to 1975 and a radio, film and television actor. Born in Tampico, Illinois and raised in Dixon, Reagan was educated at Eureka College, earning a Bachelor of Arts degree in economics and sociology. After his graduation, Reagan moved first to Iowa to work as a radio broadcaster and then in to Los Angeles, California in 1937 where he began a career as an actor, first in films and later television. Some of his most notable films include Knute Rockne, All American, Kings Row, and Bedtime for Bonzo. Reagan served as president of the Screen Actors Guild, and later as a spokesman for General Electric (GE); his start in politics occurred during his work for GE. Originally a member of the Democratic Party, his positions began shifting rightward in the late 1950s, and he switched to the Republican Party in 1962. After delivering a rousing speech in support of Barry Goldwater's presidential candidacy in 1964, he was persuaded to seek the California governorship, winning two years later and again in 1970. He was defeated in his run for the Republican presidential nomination in 1968 as well as 1976, but won both the nomination and election in 1980, defeating incumbent Jimmy Carter. As president, Reagan implemented sweeping new political and economic initiatives. His supply-side economic policies, dubbed 'Reaganomics', advocated reducing tax rates to spur economic growth, controlling the money supply to reduce inflation, deregulation of the economy, and reducing government spending. In his first term he survived an assassination attempt, took a hard line against labor unions, and ordered an invasion of Grenada. He was reelected in a landslide in 1984, proclaiming that it was 'Morning in America.' His second term was primarily marked by foreign matters, such as the ending of the Cold War, the 1986 bombing of Libya, and the revelation of the Iran-Contra affair. Publicly describing the Soviet Union as an 'evil empire,' he supported anti-communist movements worldwide and spent his first term forgoing the strategy of détente by ordering a massive military buildup in an arms race with the USSR. Reagan negotiated with Soviet General Secretary Mikhail Gorbachev, culminating in the INF Treaty and the decrease of both countries' nuclear arsenals. Reagan left office in 1989. In 1994, the former president disclosed that he had been diagnosed with Alzheimer's disease earlier in the year; he died ten years later at the age of 93. He ranks highly in public opinion polls of U.S. Presidents and is credited for generating an ideological renaissance on the American political right. Early life Ronald Wilson Reagan was born in an apartment on the second floor of a commercial building in Tampico, Illinois on February 6, 1911, to Jack Reagan and Nelle Wilson Reagan.

Reagan's father was a salesman and a storyteller, the grandson of Irish Catholic immigrants from County Tipperary while his mother had Scots and English ancestors. Reagan had one sibling, his older brother, Neil (1908-1996), who became an advertising executive. As a boy, Reagan's father nicknamed his son 'Dutch', due to his 'fat little Dutchman'-like appearance, and his 'Dutchboy' haircut; the nickname stuck with him throughout his youth. Reagan's family briefly lived in several towns and cities in Illinois, including Monmouth, Galesburg and Chicago, until 1919, when they returned to Tampico and lived above the H.C. Pitney Variety Store. After his election as president, residing in the upstairs White House private quarters, Reagan would quip that he was 'living above the store again'.

According to Paul Kengor, author of God and Ronald Reagan, Reagan had a particularly strong faith in the goodness of people, which stemmed from the optimistic faith of his mother, Nelle, and the Disciples of Christ faith, which he was baptized into in 1922. For the time, Reagan was unusual in his opposition to racial discrimination, and recalled a time in Dixon when the local inn would not allow black people to stay there.

Mechanism	The term Social mechanisms and mechanism-based explanations of social phenomenon originate from the philosophy of science. The core idea behind the mechanism approach has been expressed as follows by Elster (1989: 3-4): 'To explain an event is to give an account of why it happened. Usually... this takes the form of citing an earlier event as the cause of the event we want to explain....
Discovery	Discovery is the act of detecting something new, or something 'old' that had been unknown. With reference to science and academic disciplines, discovery is the observation of new phenomena, new actions, or new events and providing new reasoning to explain the knowledge gathered through such observations with previously acquired knowledge from abstract thought and everyday experiences. Visual discoveries are often called sightings.
Drug user	A drug user is a person who uses drugs either legally or illegally. The term user is typically employed more to refer to illegal drug use by a person who is often part of a subculture of recreational drug use. Drug users are often referred to as 'heads', depending on the drug used, i.e., pothead, hophead, crackhead, etc.
Homeland security	Homeland security is an umbrella term for security efforts to protect states against terrorist activity. Specifically, is a concerted national effort to prevent terrorist attacks within the U.S., reduce America's vulnerability to terrorism, and minimize the damage and recover from attacks that do occur. The term arose following a reorganization of many U.S.

6. Stimulants

Physical dependence	Physical dependence refers to a state resulting from chronic use of a drug that has produced tolerance and where negative physical symptoms of withdrawal result from abrupt discontinuation or dosage reduction. Physical dependence can develop from low-dose therapeutic use of certain medications such as benzodiazepines, opioids, antiepileptics and antidepressants, as well as misuse of recreational drugs such as alcohol, opioids and benzodiazepines. The higher the dose used, the greater the duration of use, and the earlier age use began are predictive of worsened physical dependence and thus more severe withdrawal syndromes.
Monitoring	In medicine, monitoring is the evaluation of a disease or condition over time. It can be performed by continuously measuring certain parameters (for example, by continuously measuring vital signs by a bedside monitor), and/or by repeatedly performing medical tests (such as blood glucose monitoring in people with diabetes mellitus). Transmitting data from a monitor to a distant monitoring station is known as telemetry or biotelemetry.
Smuggling	Smuggling is the clandestine transportation of goods or persons, such as out of a building, into a prison, or across an international border, in violation of applicable laws or other regulations. There are various motivations to smuggle. These include the participation in illegal trade, such as in the drug trade, in illegal immigration or illegal emigration, tax evasion, providing contraband to a prison inmate, or the theft of the items being smuggled.
Adderall	Adderall is a brand-name psychostimulant medication composed of racemic amphetamine aspartate monohydrate, racemic amphetamine sulfate, dextroamphetamine saccharide, and dextroamphetamine sulfate, which is thought by scientists to work by increasing the amount of dopamine and norepinephrine in the brain. In addition, the drug also acts as a potent dopamine reuptake inhibitor and norepinephrine reuptake inhibitor. Adderall is widely reported to increase alertness, increase libido, increase concentration and overall cognitive performance, and, in general, improve mood, while decreasing user fatigue.
Benzedrine	Benzedrine is the trade name of the racemic mixture of amphetamine (dl-amphetamine). It was marketed under this brandname in the USA by Smith, Kline & French in the form of inhalers, starting in 1928. Benzedrine was used to enlarge nasal and bronchial passages and it is closely related to other stimulants produced later, such as dextroamphetamine (d-amphetamine) and methamphetamine. Benzedrine should not be confused with the fundamentally different substance benzphetamine.
Amotivational syndrome	Amotivational syndrome is a psychological condition associated with diminished inspiration to participate in social situations and activities, with lapses in apathy caused by an external event, situation, substance , relationship , or other cause.

While some have claimed that chronic use of cannabis causes amotivational syndrome in some users, empirical studies suggest that there is no such thing as 'amotivational syndrome', per se. From a World Health Organization report:

A study done by researchers Barnwell, Earleywine and Wilcox on a sample of undergraduates also suggests that cannabis use does not cause an amotivational syndrome.

Amphetamine	Amphetamine or amfetamine (INN) is a psychostimulant drug of the phenethylamine class which produces increased wakefulness and focus in association with decreased fatigue and appetite.

Brand names of medications that contain, or metabolize into, amphetamine include Adderall, Dexedrine, Dextrostat, Desoxyn, ProCentra, and Vyvanse, as well as Benzedrine in the past.

The drug is also used recreationally and as a performance enhancer. |
| Alcohol dependence | Alcohol dependence is a psychiatric diagnosis (a substance related disorder DSM-IV) describing an entity in which an individual uses alcohol despite significant areas of dysfunction, evidence of physical dependence, and/or related hardship, and also may cause stress and bipolar disorder.

According to the DSM-IV criteria for alcohol dependence, at least three out of seven of the following criteria must be manifest during a 12 month period:•Tolerance•Withdrawal symptoms or clinically defined Alcohol Withdrawal Syndrome•Use in larger amounts or for longer periods than intended•Persistent desire or unsuccessful efforts to cut down on alcohol use•Time is spent obtaining alcohol or recovering from effects•Social, occupational and recreational pursuits are given up or reduced because of alcohol use•Use is continued despite knowledge of alcohol-related harm (physical or psychological)History and epidemiology

About 12% of American adults have had an alcohol dependence problem at some time in their life. The term 'alcohol dependence' has replaced 'alcoholism' as a term in order that individuals do not internalize the idea of cure and disease, but can approach alcohol as a chemical they may depend upon to cope with outside pressures. |
| Heroin | Heroin (diacetylmorphine or morphine diacetate (INN)), also known as diamorphine (BAN), is an opiate analgesic synthesized by C.R Alder Wright in 1874 by adding two acetyl groups to the molecule morphine, a derivative of the opium poppy. When used in medicine it is typically used to treat severe pain, such as that resulting from a heart attack. It is the 3,6-diacetyl ester of morphine, and functions as a morphine prodrug (meaning that it is metabolically converted to morphine inside the body in order for it to work). |
| Inheritance | Inheritance is the practice of passing on property, titles, debts, rights and obligations upon the death of an individual. It represents also to pass a characteristic, genetically. |

6. Stimulants

Methamphetamine	Methamphetamine is a psychostimulant of the phenethylamine and amphetamine class of drugs. It increases alertness, concentration, energy, and in high doses, can induce euphoria, enhances self-esteem, and increase libido. Methamphetamine has high potential for abuse and addiction by activating the psychological reward system via triggering a cascading release of dopamine and norepinephrine in the brain.
Dopamine	Dopamine is a catecholamine neurotransmitter present in a wide variety of animals, including both vertebrates and invertebrates. In the brain, this substituted phenethylamine functions as a neurotransmitter, activating the five known types of dopamine receptors--D_1, D_2, D_3, D_4, and D_5--and their variants. Dopamine is produced in several areas of the brain, including the substantia nigra and the ventral tegmental area.
Monoamine neurotransmitter	Monoamine neurotransmitters are neurotransmitters and neuromodulators that contain one amino group that is connected to an aromatic ring by a two-carbon chain ($-CH_2-CH_2-$). All monoamines are derived from aromatic amino acids like phenylalanine, tyrosine, tryptophan, and the thyroid hormones by the action of aromatic amino acid decarboxylase enzymes.
Psilocybin	Psilocybin is a naturally occurring psychedelic compound produced by over 200 species of mushrooms, collectively known as psilocybin mushrooms. The most potent are members of the genus Psilocybe, such as P. azurescens, P. semilanceata, and P. cyanescens, but psilocybin has also been isolated from about a dozen other genera. As a prodrug, psilocybin is quickly converted by the body to psilocin, which has mind-altering effects similar to those of LSD and mescaline.
Absorption	In economics, absorption is the total demand for all final marketed goods and services by all economic agents resident in an economy, regardless of the origin of the goods and services themselves. As the absorption is equal to the sum of all domestically-produced goods consumed locally and all imports, it is equal to national income [Y = C + I + G + (X - M)] minus the balance of trade [X - M]. The term was coined, and its relation to the balance of trade identified, by Sidney Alexander in 1952.
Prescription	In law, prescription is the method of sovereignty transfer of a territory through international law analogous to the common law doctrine of adverse possession for private real-estate. Prescription involves the open encroachment by the new sovereign upon the territory in question for a prolonged period of time, acting as the sovereign, without protest or other contest by the original sovereign. This doctrine legalizes de jure the de facto transfer of sovereignty caused in part by the original sovereign's extended negligence and/or neglect of the area in question.
Paranoia	Since 1992, Paranoia: The Conspiracy & Paranormal Reader has presented alternative views and marginalized theories of the inner workings of the cryptocracy. Subjects include conspiracy theories, parapolitics, alternative history, and the paranormal.

Stimulation	Stimulation is the action of various agents (stimuli) on nerves, muscles, or a sensory end organ, by which activity is evoked; especially, the nervous impulse produced by various agents on nerves, or a sensory end organ, by which the part connected with the nerve is thrown into a state of activity.
	The word is also often used metaphorically. For example, an interesting or fun activity can be described as 'stimulating', regardless of its physical effects on nerves.

CHAPTER QUIZ: KEY TERMS, PEOPLE, PLACES, CONCEPTS

1. The term Social _____s and _____-based explanations of social phenomenon originate from the philosophy of science.

   The core idea behind the _____ approach has been expressed as follows by Elster (1989: 3-4): 'To explain an event is to give an account of why it happened. Usually... this takes the form of citing an earlier event as the cause of the event we want to explain....

   a. Memetic institutionalism
   b. Mechanism
   c. Meta-power
   d. Middleman minority

2. _____ is a 1922 British crime film directed by Graham Cutts and starring Hilda Bayley, Flora Le Breton, Ward McAllister and Cyril Raymond. A melodrama - it depicts the distribution of _____ by gangsters through a series of London nightclubs and the revenge sought by a man after the death of his daughter.

   Because of its depiction of drug use, it was the most controversial British film of the 1920s.

   a. Cocaine
   b. The Embezzler
   c. The Flying Scot
   d. Gangs of New York

3. . _____ refers to a state resulting from chronic use of a drug that has produced tolerance and where negative physical symptoms of withdrawal result from abrupt discontinuation or dosage reduction. _____ can develop from low-dose therapeutic use of certain medications such as benzodiazepines, opioids, antiepileptics and antidepressants, as well as misuse of recreational drugs such as alcohol, opioids and benzodiazepines. The higher the dose used, the greater the duration of use, and the earlier age use began are predictive of worsened _____ and thus more severe withdrawal syndromes.

6. Stimulants

   a. Character disorder
   b. Physical dependence
   c. La Guardia Committee
   d. Las Vegas Jailhouse

4. _____ or amfetamine (INN) is a psychostimulant drug of the phenethylamine class which produces increased wakefulness and focus in association with decreased fatigue and appetite.

   Brand names of medications that contain, or metabolize into, _____ include Adderall, Dexedrine, Dextrostat, Desoxyn, ProCentra, and Vyvanse, as well as Benzedrine in the past.

   The drug is also used recreationally and as a performance enhancer.

   a. Antonio Commisso
   b. Amphetamine
   c. Apathy
   d. Eating disorder

5. _____ is the practice of passing on property, titles, debts, rights and obligations upon the death of an individual. It represents also to pass a characteristic, genetically. It has long played an important role in human societies.

   a. Ademption
   b. Inheritance
   c. Agnatic seniority
   d. Ancillary administration

1. b
2. a
3. b
4. b
5. b

You can take the complete Chapter Practice Test

for 6. Stimulants
on all key terms, persons, places, and concepts.

Online 99 Cents

http://www.epub4.1.22005.6.cram101.com/

Use www.Cram101.com for all your study needs

including Cram101's online interactive problem solving labs in

chemistry, statistics, mathematics, and more.

7. Depressants and Inhalants

CHAPTER OUTLINE: KEY TERMS, PEOPLE, PLACES, CONCEPTS

	Benzedrine
	Barbiturate
	Benzodiazepine
	Identity
	Mechanism
	Mickey Finn
	Amobarbital
	Chloral hydrate
	Secobarbital
	Duration
	Controlled substance
	Meprobamate
	Drug user
	Lethal injection
	Social influence
	Substance abuse
	Cocaine
	Physical dependence
	Psychological dependence
	Zaleplon
	Agent

Codeine

Tablet

Punishment

Anxiety

Behaviour therapy

Obsessive-compulsive personality disorder

Phobia

Anxiety disorder

Triazolam

Amotivational syndrome

Production

Xyrem

Cataplexy

Benzedrine	Benzedrine is the trade name of the racemic mixture of amphetamine (dl-amphetamine). It was marketed under this brandname in the USA by Smith, Kline & French in the form of inhalers, starting in 1928. Benzedrine was used to enlarge nasal and bronchial passages and it is closely related to other stimulants produced later, such as dextroamphetamine (d-amphetamine) and methamphetamine. Benzedrine should not be confused with the fundamentally different substance benzphetamine.
Barbiturate	Barbiturates are drugs that act as central nervous system depressants, and, by virtue of this, they produce a wide spectrum of effects, from mild sedation to total anesthesia. They are also effective as anxiolytics, as hypnotics, and as anticonvulsants. They have addiction potential, both physical and psychological.
Benzodiazepine	A benzodiazepine is a psychoactive drug whose core chemical structure is the fusion of a benzene ring and a diazepine ring. The first benzodiazepine, chlordiazepoxide (Librium), was discovered accidentally by Leo Sternbach in 1955, and made available in 1960 by Hoffmann-La Roche, which has also marketed diazepam (Valium) since 1963. Benzodiazepines enhance the effect of the neurotransmitter gamma-aminobutyric acid (GABA), which results in sedative, hypnotic (sleep-inducing), anxiolytic (anti-anxiety), anticonvulsant, muscle relaxant and amnesic action.
Identity	Identity is a term used to describe a person's conception and expression of their individuality or group affiliations (such as national identity and cultural identity). The term is used more specifically in psychology and sociology, and is given a great deal of attention in social psychology. The term is also used with respect to place identity.
Mechanism	The term Social mechanisms and mechanism-based explanations of social phenomenon originate from the philosophy of science. The core idea behind the mechanism approach has been expressed as follows by Elster (1989: 3-4): 'To explain an event is to give an account of why it happened. Usually... this takes the form of citing an earlier event as the cause of the event we want to explain....
Mickey Finn	A Mickey Finn is a slang term for a drink laced with a drug (especially chloral hydrate) given to someone without their knowledge in order to incapacitate them. Serving someone a Mickey Finn is most commonly referred to as slipping a mickey, sometimes spelled 'slipping a mickie'. History of term The Chicago bartender Michael 'Mickey' Finn

7. Depressants and Inhalants

Amobarbital	Amobarbital is a drug that is a barbiturate derivative. It has sedative-hypnotic properties. It is a white crystalline powder with no odor and a slightly bitter taste.
Chloral hydrate	Chloral hydrate is a sedative and hypnotic drug as well as a chemical reagent and precursor. The name chloral hydrate indicates that it is formed from chloral (trichloroacetaldehyde) by the addition of one molecule of water. Its chemical formula is $C_2H_3Cl_3O_2$.
Secobarbital	Secobarbital sodium (marketed by Eli Lilly and Company, and subsequently by other companies as described below, under the brand name Seconal) is a barbiturate derivative drug that was first synthesized in 1928 in Germany. It possesses anaesthetic, anticonvulsant, sedative and hypnotic properties. In the United Kingdom, it was known as Quinalbarbitone.
Duration	Duration is a theory of time and consciousness posited by the French philosopher Henri Bergson. Bergson sought to improve upon inadequacies he perceived in the philosophy of Herbert Spencer, due, he believed, to Spencer's lack of comprehension of mechanics, which led Bergson to the conclusion that time eluded mathematics and science. Bergson became aware that the moment one attempted to measure a moment, it would be gone: one measures an immobile, complete line, whereas time is mobile and incomplete.
Controlled substance	A controlled substance is generally a drug or chemical whose manufacture, possession, and use are regulated by a government. This may include illegal drugs and prescription medications (designated Controlled Drug in the United Kingdom).
Meprobamate	Meprobamate is a carbamate derivative which is used as an anxiolytic drug. It was the best-selling minor tranquilizer for a time, but has largely been replaced by the benzodiazepines. History Meprobamate was first synthesized by Bernard John Ludwig, PhD, and Frank Milan Berger, MD, at Carter Products in May 1950. Wallace Laboratories, a subsidiary of Carter Products, bought the license and named it Miltown after the borough of Milltown in New Jersey.
Drug user	A drug user is a person who uses drugs either legally or illegally. The term user is typically employed more to refer to illegal drug use by a person who is often part of a subculture of recreational drug use. Drug users are often referred to as 'heads' depending on the drug used, i.e., pothead, hophead, crackhead, etc.
Lethal injection	Lethal injection is the practice of injecting a person with a fatal dose of drugs (typically a barbiturate, paralytic, and potassium solution) for the express purpose of causing the immediate death of the subject. The main application for this procedure is capital punishment, but the term may also be applied in a broad sense to euthanasia and suicide.

Social influence	Social influence occurs when one's emotions, opinions, or behaviors are affected by others. Social influence takes many forms and can be seen in conformity, socialization, peer pressure, obedience, leadership, persuasion, sales, and marketing. In 1958, Harvard psychologist, Herbert Kelman identified three broad varieties of social influence.
Substance abuse	Substance abuse, also known as drug abuse, is a patterned use of a substance (drug) in which the user consumes the substance in amounts or with methods neither approved nor supervised by medical professionals. Substance abuse/drug abuse is not limited to mood-altering or psycho-active drugs. If an activity is performed using the objects against the rules and policies of the matter (as in steroids for performance enhancement in sports), it is also called substance abuse.
Cocaine	Cocaine is a 1922 British crime film directed by Graham Cutts and starring Hilda Bayley, Flora Le Breton, Ward McAllister and Cyril Raymond. A melodrama - it depicts the distribution of cocaine by gangsters through a series of London nightclubs and the revenge sought by a man after the death of his daughter. Because of its depiction of drug use, it was the most controversial British film of the 1920s.
Physical dependence	Physical dependence refers to a state resulting from chronic use of a drug that has produced tolerance and where negative physical symptoms of withdrawal result from abrupt discontinuation or dosage reduction. Physical dependence can develop from low-dose therapeutic use of certain medications such as benzodiazepines, opioids, antiepileptics and antidepressants, as well as misuse of recreational drugs such as alcohol, opioids and benzodiazepines. The higher the dose used, the greater the duration of use, and the earlier age use began are predictive of worsened physical dependence and thus more severe withdrawal syndromes.
Psychological dependence	In the APA Dictionary of Psychology, psychological dependence is defined as 'dependence on a psychoactive substance for the reinforcement it provides.' Most times psychological dependence is classified under addiction. They are similar in that addiction is a physiological 'craving' for something and psychological dependence is a 'need' for a particular substance because it causes enjoyable mental affects. A person becomes dependent on something to help alleviate specific emotions.
Zaleplon	Zaleplon is a sedative/hypnotic, mainly used for insomnia. It is a nonbenzodiazepine hypnotic from the pyrazolopyrimidine class. In terms of adverse effects zaleplon appears to offer little improvement compared to both benzodiazepines and other non-benzodiazepine Z-drugs.
Agent	In economics, an agent is an actor and decision maker in a model. Typically, every agent makes decisions by solving a well or ill defined optimization/choice problem. The term agent can also be seen as equivalent to player in game theory.

7. Depressants and Inhalants

Codeine	Codeine or 3-methylmorphine (a natural isomer of methylated morphine, the other being the semi-synthetic 6-methylmorphine) is an opiate used for its analgesic, antitussive, and antidiarrheal properties. Codeine is the second-most predominant alkaloid in opium, at up to 3 percent; it is much more prevalent in the Iranian poppy (Papaver bractreatum), and codeine is extracted from this species in some places although the below-mentioned morphine methylation process is still much more common. It is considered the prototype of the weak to midrange opioids.
Tablet	A tablet is a pharmaceutical dosage form. It comprises a mixture of active substances and excipients, usually in powder form, pressed or compacted from a powder into a solid dose. The excipients can include diluents, binders or granulating agents, glidants (flow aids) and lubricants to ensure efficient tabletting; disintegrants to promote tablet break-up in the digestive tract; sweeteners or flavours to enhance taste; and pigments to make the tablets visually attractive.
Punishment	In operant conditioning, punishment is any change in a human or animal's surroundings that occurs after a given behavior or response which reduces the likelihood of that behavior occurring again in the future. As with reinforcement, it is the behavior, not the animal, that is punished. Whether a change is or is not punishing is only known by its effect on the rate of the behavior, not by any 'hostile' or aversive features of the change.
Anxiety	Anxiety is a psychological and physiological state characterized by somatic, emotional, cognitive, and behavioral components. It is the displeasing feeling of fear and concern. The root meaning of the word anxiety is 'to vex or trouble'; in either presence or absence of psychological stress, anxiety can create feelings of fear, worry, uneasiness, and dread.
Behaviour therapy	Behaviour therapy is an approach to psychotherapy in the behaviourism tradition that focuses on a set of methods designed for reinforcing desired and eliminating undesired behaviors without concerning itself with the psychoanalytic state of the subject. In its broadest sense the methods focus on behaviors not the thoughts and feelings that might be causing them. Behavior therapy breaks down into two disciplines, a more narrowly defined sense of behavior therapy and behavior modification.
Obsessive-compulsive personality disorder	Obsessive-compulsive personality disorder is a personality disorder characterized by a pervasive pattern of preoccupation with orderliness, perfectionism, and mental and interpersonal control at the expense of flexibility, openness, and efficiency. The primary symptoms of obsessive\ compulsive\ personality\ disorder can include preoccupation with remembering and paying attention to minute details and facts, following rules and regulations, compulsion to make lists and schedules, as well as rigidity/inflexibility of beliefs and/or exhibition of perfectionism that interferes with task-completion. Symptoms may cause extreme distress and interfere with a person's occupational and social functioning. According to the National Institute for Mental Health:

Most patients spend their early life avoiding symptoms and developing techniques to avoid dealing with these strenuous issues. Obsession

Some, but not all, patients with obsessive\ compulsive\ personality\ disorder show an obsessive need for cleanliness. This obsessive\ compulsive\ personality\ disorder trait is not to be confused with domestic efficiency; over-attention to related details may instead make these (and other) activities of daily living difficult to accomplish. Though obsessive behavior is in part a way to control anxiety, tension often remains. In the case of a hoarder, attention effectively to clean the home may be hindered by the amount of clutter that the hoarder resolves later to organize.

While there are superficial similarities between the list-making and obsessive aspects of Asperger's syndrome and obsessive\ compulsive\ personality\ disorder, the former is different from obsessive\ compulsive\ personality\ disorder especially regarding affective behaviors, including (but not limited to) empathy, social coping, and general social skills.

Perception of own and others' actions and beliefs tend to be polarised (i.e., 'right' or 'wrong', with little or no margin between the two) for people with this disorder. As might be expected, such rigidity places strain on interpersonal relationships, with frustration sometimes turning into anger and even violence. This is known as disinhibition. People with obsessive\ compulsive\ personality\ disorder often tend to general pessimism and/or underlying form(s) of depression. This can at times become so serious that suicide is a risk. Indeed, one study suggests that personality disorders are a significant substrate to psychiatric morbidity. They may cause more problems in functioning than a major depressive episode. Causes

Research into the familial tendency of obsessive\ compulsive\ personality\ disorder may be illuminated by DNA studies. Two studies suggest that people with a particular form of the DRD3 gene are highly likely to develop obsessive\ compulsive\ personality\ disorder and depression, particularly if they are male. Genetic concomitants, however, may lie dormant until triggered by events in the lives of those who are predisposed to obsessive\ compulsive\ personality\ disorder. These events could include trauma faced during childhood, such as physical, emotional or sexual abuse, or other types of psychological trauma. Diagnosis DSM

The Diagnostic and Statistical Manual of Mental Disorders fourth edition, (DSM IV-TR = 301.4), a widely used manual for diagnosing mental disorders, defines obsessive-compulsive personality disorder (in Axis II Cluster C) as:A pervasive pattern of preoccupation with orderliness, perfectionism, and mental and interpersonal control, at the expense of flexibility, openness, and efficiency, beginning by early adulthood and present in a variety of contexts. It is a requirement of DSM-IV that a diagnosis of any specific personality disorder also satisfies a set of general personality disorder criteria.Criticism

7. Depressants and Inhalants

Since DSM IV-TR was published in 2000, some studies have found fault with its obsessive\ compulsive\ personality\ disorder coverage. A 2004 study challenged the usefulness of all but three of the criteria: perfectionism, rigidity and stubbornness, and miserliness. A study in 2007 found that obsessive\ compulsive\ personality\ disorder is etiologically distinct from avoidant and dependent personality disorders, suggesting it is incorrectly categorized as a Cluster C disorder. WHO

The World Health Organization's ICD-10 uses the term (F60.5) Anankastic personality disorder. It is characterized by at least three of the following:•feelings of excessive doubt and caution;•preoccupation with details, rules, lists, order, organization or schedule;•perfectionism that interferes with task completion;•excessive conscientiousness, scrupulousness, and undue preoccupation with productivity to the exclusion of pleasure and interpersonal relationships;•excessive pedantry and adherence to social conventions;•rigidity and stubbornness;•unreasonable insistence by the individual that others submit exactly to his or her way of doing things, or unreasonable reluctance to allow others to do things;•intrusion of insistent and unwelcome thoughts or impulses.Includes: •compulsive and obsessional personality (disorder)•obsessive-compulsive personality disorderExcludes: •obsessive-compulsive disorder

It is a requirement of ICD-10 that a diagnosis of any specific personality disorder also satisfies a set of general personality disorder criteria.

Phobia

A phobia is, when used in the context of clinical psychology, a type of anxiety disorder, usually defined as a persistent fear of an object or situation in which the sufferer commits to great lengths in avoiding, typically disproportional to the actual danger posed, often being recognized as irrational. In the event the phobia cannot be avoided entirely, the sufferer will endure the situation or object with marked distress and significant interference in social or occupational activities.

The terms distress and impairment as defined by the Diagnostic and Statistical Manual of Mental Disorders, Fourth Edition (DSM-IV-TR) should also take into account the context of the sufferer's environment if attempting a diagnosis.

Anxiety disorder

Anxiety disorder is a blanket term covering several different forms of a type of mental illness of abnormal and pathological fear and anxiety. Conditions now considered anxiety disorders only came under the aegis of psychiatry near the end of the 19th century. Gelder, Mayou & Geddes (2005) explain that anxiety disorders are classified in two groups: continuous symptoms and episodic symptoms.

Triazolam

Triazolam is a benzodiazepine drug. It possesses pharmacological properties similar to that of other benzodiazepines, but it is generally only used as a sedative to treat severe insomnia. In addition to the hypnotic properties triazolam possesses, amnesic, anxiolytic, sedative, anticonvulsant and muscle relaxant properties are also present.

Amotivational syndrome	Amotivational syndrome is a psychological condition associated with diminished inspiration to participate in social situations and activities, with lapses in apathy caused by an external event, situation, substance , relationship , or other cause.

While some have claimed that chronic use of cannabis causes amotivational syndrome in some users, empirical studies suggest that there is no such thing as 'amotivational syndrome', per se. From a World Health Organization report:

A study done by researchers Barnwell, Earleywine and Wilcox on a sample of undergraduates also suggests that cannabis use does not cause an amotivational syndrome. |
| Production | In economics, production is the act of creating output, a good or service which has value and contributes to the utility of individuals. The act may or may not include factors of production other than labor. Any effort directed toward the realization of a desired product or service is a 'productive' effort and the performance of such act is production. |
| Xyrem | Xyrem is a prescription medication manufactured by Jazz Pharmaceuticals, and is approved by the U.S. Food and Drug Administration (FDA) for the treatment of cataplexy associated with narcolepsy and Excessive Daytime Sleepiness (EDS) associated with narcolepsy. Sodium oxybate is the sodium salt of γ-hydroxybutyric acid.

The American Academy of Sleep Medicine (AASM) recommends Xyrem as a standard of care for the treatment of cataplexy, daytime sleepiness, and disrupted sleep due to narcolepsy in its Practice Parameters for the Treatment of Narcolepsy and other Hypersomnias of Central Origin. |
| Cataplexy | Cataplexy is a sudden and transient episode of loss of muscle tone, often triggered by emotions. It is a rare disease (prevalence of fewer than 5 per 10,000 in the community), but affects roughly 70% of people who have narcolepsy. Cataplexy can also be present as a side effect of SSRI Discontinuation Syndrome. |

7. Depressants and Inhalants

1. _____ is a theory of time and consciousness posited by the French philosopher Henri Bergson. Bergson sought to improve upon inadequacies he perceived in the philosophy of Herbert Spencer, due, he believed, to Spencer's lack of comprehension of mechanics, which led Bergson to the conclusion that time eluded mathematics and science. Bergson became aware that the moment one attempted to measure a moment, it would be gone: one measures an immobile, complete line, whereas time is mobile and incomplete.

   a. Free will in antiquity
   b. Free will in theology
   c. Free will theorem
   d. Duration

2. _____ is the trade name of the racemic mixture of amphetamine (dl-amphetamine). It was marketed under this brandname in the USA by Smith, Kline & French in the form of inhalers, starting in 1928. _____ was used to enlarge nasal and bronchial passages and it is closely related to other stimulants produced later, such as dextroamphetamine (d-amphetamine) and methamphetamine. _____ should not be confused with the fundamentally different substance benzphetamine.

   a. Visa overstay
   b. withdrawl
   c. Benzedrine
   d. Cosimo Commisso

3. _____ is a prescription medication manufactured by Jazz Pharmaceuticals, and is approved by the U.S. Food and Drug Administration (FDA) for the treatment of cataplexy associated with narcolepsy and Excessive Daytime Sleepiness (EDS) associated with narcolepsy. Sodium oxybate is the sodium salt of γ-hydroxybutyric acid.

   The American Academy of Sleep Medicine (AASM) recommends _____ as a standard of care for the treatment of cataplexy, daytime sleepiness, and disrupted sleep due to narcolepsy in its Practice Parameters for the Treatment of Narcolepsy and other Hypersomnias of Central Origin.

   a. Sundowning
   b. Thai Ngoc
   c. Xyrem
   d. VPIN

4. . _____ is a psychological and physiological state characterized by somatic, emotional, cognitive, and behavioral components. It is the displeasing feeling of fear and concern. The root meaning of the word _____ is 'to vex or trouble'; in either presence or absence of psychological stress, _____ can create feelings of fear, worry, uneasiness, and dread.

   a. Essence
   b. Antonio Commisso
   c. Antonio Imerti

Visit Cram101.com for full Practice Exams

5. _____ is a 1922 British crime film directed by Graham Cutts and starring Hilda Bayley, Flora Le Breton, Ward McAllister and Cyril Raymond. A melodrama - it depicts the distribution of _____ by gangsters through a series of London nightclubs and the revenge sought by a man after the death of his daughter.

Because of its depiction of drug use, it was the most controversial British film of the 1920s.

a. Deadlock
b. The Embezzler
c. The Flying Scot
d. Cocaine

1. d
2. c
3. c
4. d
5. d

You can take the complete Chapter Practice Test

for 7. Depressants and Inhalants
on all key terms, persons, places, and concepts.

Online 99 Cents

http://www.epub4.1.22005.7.cram101.com/

Use www.Cram101.com for all your study needs

including Cram101's online interactive problem solving labs in

chemistry, statistics, mathematics, and more.

	Medicare
	Mental disorder
	Relocation
	Nursing home
	Patent medicine
	Prescription
	Substance abuse
	Diversion
	Anxiety
	Anxiety disorder
	Chemical imbalance
	Cocaine
	Codeine
	Direct evidence
	Liver
	Frontal lobe
	Agoraphobia
	Bipolar disorder
	Controlled substance
	Depression
	Generalized anxiety disorder

_____ | Meprobamate

_____ | Mood disorder

_____ | Obsessive-compulsive personality disorder

_____ | Panic attack

_____ | Panic disorder

_____ | Phobia

_____ | Social influence

_____ | Specific phobia

_____ | Lethal injection

_____ | Schizophrenia

_____ | Punishment

_____ | Electroconvulsive therapy

_____ | Scientific evidence

_____ | Tracking

_____ | Chlorpromazine

_____ | Mechanism

_____ | Outcome

_____ | Phenothiazine

_____ | Refusal skills

_____ | Blocking

_____ | Production

	Side Effects
	Intervention
	Agent
	Amphetamine
	Diabetes
	Representation
	Survivors guilt
	Monitoring
	Monoamine oxidase
	Categories
	Drug possession
	Binge drinking
	Liberation

8. Medication for Mental Disorders

Medicare	Medicare is a national social insurance program, administered by the U.S. federal government in 1965, that guarantees access to health insurance for Americans ages 65 and older and younger people with disabilities as well as people with end stage renal disease. As a social insurance program, Medicare spreads the financial risk associated with illness across society to protect everyone, and thus has a somewhat different social role from private insurers, which must manage their risk portfolio to guarantee their own solvency. Medicare offers all enrollees a defined benefit.
Mental disorder	A mental disorder or mental illness is a psychological pattern or anomaly, potentially reflected in behavior, that is generally associated with distress or disability, and which is not considered part of normal development of a person's culture. Mental disorders are generally defined by a combination of how a person feels, acts, thinks or perceives. This may be associated with particular regions or functions of the brain or rest of the nervous system, often in a social context.
Relocation	Relocation is the process of vacating a fixed location (such as a residence or business) and settling in a different one. A move can be to a nearby location within the same neighborhood, a much farther location in a different city, or sometimes a different country. On the Holmes and Rahe stress scale for adults, 'change of residence' is considered a stressful activity, assigned 20 points (with death of spouse being ranked the highest at 100), although other changes on the scale (e.g. 'change in living conditions', 'change in social activities') often occur as a result of relocating, making the overall stress level potentially higher.
Nursing home	A nursing home, convalescent home, Skilled Nursing Unit (SNU), care home or rest home provides a type of care of residents: it is a place of residence for people who require constant nursing care and have significant deficiencies with activities of daily living. Residents include the elderly and younger adults with physical or mental disabilities. Residents in a skilled nursing facility may also receive physical, occupational, and other rehabilitative therapies following an accident or illness.
Patent medicine	Patent medicine refers to medical compounds of questionable effectiveness sold under a variety of names and labels. The term 'patent medicine' is somewhat of a misnomer because, in most cases, although many of the products were trademarked, they were never patented (most avoided the patent process so as not to reveal products' often hazardous and questionable ingredients). Perhaps the only 'patent medicine' ever to be patented was Castoria.
Prescription	In law, prescription is the method of sovereignty transfer of a territory through international law analogous to the common law doctrine of adverse possession for private real-estate. Prescription involves the open encroachment by the new sovereign upon the territory in question for a prolonged period of time, acting as the sovereign, without protest or other contest by the original sovereign. This doctrine legalizes de jure the de facto transfer of sovereignty caused in part by the original sovereign's extended negligence and/or neglect of the area in question.

Substance abuse	Substance abuse, also known as drug abuse, is a patterned use of a substance (drug) in which the user consumes the substance in amounts or with methods neither approved nor supervised by medical professionals. Substance abuse/drug abuse is not limited to mood-altering or psycho-active drugs. If an activity is performed using the objects against the rules and policies of the matter (as in steroids for performance enhancement in sports), it is also called substance abuse.
Diversion	Diversion may refer to:•diversion, a detour, especially of an airplane flight due to severe weather or mechanical failure, or of an ambulance from a fully occupied emergency room to one another nearby hospital•diversion, a distraction•diversion, a form of logical fallacy known as a general irrelevancy, a violation of sound reasoning•diversion, the rerouting of water from a river or lake for flood control, or as part of a water supply network for drinking water or irrigation •Diversion, a British television film later adapted into the 1987 movie Fatal Attraction•Diversion program, criminal justice scheme usually for minor offenses•Diversionary tactic, also known as feint; a military deception designed to draw enemy strength away from a primary target•Pharmaceutical diversion, the diversion of licit drugs for illicit purposes•Product diversion, the sale of products in unintended markets•Yamaha Diversion, a motorcycle manufactured by Yamaha.
Anxiety	Anxiety is a psychological and physiological state characterized by somatic, emotional, cognitive, and behavioral components. It is the displeasing feeling of fear and concern. The root meaning of the word anxiety is 'to vex or trouble'; in either presence or absence of psychological stress, anxiety can create feelings of fear, worry, uneasiness, and dread.
Anxiety disorder	Anxiety disorder is a blanket term covering several different forms of a type of mental illness of abnormal and pathological fear and anxiety. Conditions now considered anxiety disorders only came under the aegis of psychiatry near the end of the 19th century. Gelder, Mayou & Geddes (2005) explain that anxiety disorders are classified in two groups: continuous symptoms and episodic symptoms.
Chemical imbalance	Chemical imbalance is one hypothesis about the cause of mental illness. Other causes that are debated include psychological and social causes. The basic concept is that neurotransmitter imbalances within the brain are the main causes of psychiatric conditions and that these conditions can be improved with medication which corrects these imbalances.
Cocaine	Cocaine is a 1922 British crime film directed by Graham Cutts and starring Hilda Bayley, Flora Le Breton, Ward McAllister and Cyril Raymond. A melodrama - it depicts the distribution of cocaine by gangsters through a series of London nightclubs and the revenge sought by a man after the death of his daughter. Because of its depiction of drug use, it was the most controversial British film of the 1920s.

8. Medication for Mental Disorders

Codeine	Codeine or 3-methylmorphine (a natural isomer of methylated morphine, the other being the semi-synthetic 6-methylmorphine) is an opiate used for its analgesic, antitussive, and antidiarrheal properties. Codeine is the second-most predominant alkaloid in opium, at up to 3 percent; it is much more prevalent in the Iranian poppy (Papaver bractreatum), and codeine is extracted from this species in some places although the below-mentioned morphine methylation process is still much more common. It is considered the prototype of the weak to midrange opioids.
Direct evidence	Direct evidence supports the truth of an assertion (in criminal law, an assertion of guilt or of innocence) directly, i.e., without an intervening inference. Circumstantial evidence, by contrast, consists of a fact or set of facts which, if proven, will support the creation of an inference that the matter asserted is true. For example: a witness who testifies that he saw the defendant shoot the victim gives direct evidence.
Liver	The liver, hepar, is a vital organ present in vertebrates and some other animals. It has a wide range of functions, including detoxification, protein synthesis, and production of biochemicals necessary for digestion. The liver is necessary for survival; there is currently no way to compensate for the absence of liver function in the long term, although new liver dialysis techniques can be used in the short term.
Frontal lobe	The frontal lobe is an area in the brain of humans and other mammals, located at the front of each cerebral hemisphere and positioned anterior to (in front of) the parietal lobe and superior and anterior to the temporal lobes. It is separated from the parietal lobe by a space between tissues called the central sulcus, and from the temporal lobe by a deep fold called the lateral (Sylvian) sulcus. The post-central gyrus, forming the posterior border of the frontal lobe, contains the primary motor cortex, which controls voluntary movements of specific body parts.
Agoraphobia	Agoraphobia is an anxiety disorder characterized by anxiety in situations where it is perceived to be difficult or embarrassing to escape. These situations can include, but are not limited to, wide-open spaces, and uncontrollable social situations such as may be met in shopping malls, airports, and on bridges. Agoraphobia is defined within the DSM-IV TR as a subset of panic disorder, involving the fear of incurring a panic attack in those environments.
Bipolar disorder	Bipolar disorder or bipolar affective disorder (historically known as manic-depressive disorder) is a psychiatric diagnosis for a mood disorder in which people experience disruptive mood swings. These encompass a frenzied state known as mania usually alternated with symptoms of depression. Bipolar disorder is defined by the presence of one or more episodes of abnormally elevated energy levels, cognition, and mood with or without one or more depressive episodes.
Controlled substance	A controlled substance is generally a drug or chemical whose manufacture, possession, and use are regulated by a government.

Depression	In economics, a depression is a sustained, long-term downturn in economic activity in one or more economies. It is a more severe downturn than a recession, which is seen by some economists as part of the modern business cycle.
	Considered by some economists to be a rare and extreme form of recession, a depression is characterized by its length; by abnormally large increases in unemployment; falls in the availability of credit, often due to some kind of banking or financial crisis; shrinking output as buyers dry up and suppliers cut back on production and investment; large number of bankruptcies including sovereign debt defaults; significantly reduced amounts of trade and commerce, especially international; as well as highly volatile relative currency value fluctuations, most often due to devaluations.
Generalized anxiety disorder	Generalized anxiety disorder is an anxiety disorder that is characterized by excessive, uncontrollable and often irrational worry about everyday things that is disproportionate to the actual source of worry. In the case of this disorder, symptoms must last at least 6 months. This excessive worry often interferes with daily functioning, as individuals suffering Generalized anxiety disorder typically anticipate disaster, and are overly concerned about everyday matters such as health issues, money, death, family problems, Friendship problems, Interpersonal relationship problems or work difficulties.
Meprobamate	Meprobamate is a carbamate derivative which is used as an anxiolytic drug. It was the best-selling minor tranquilizer for a time, but has largely been replaced by the benzodiazepines.
	History
	Meprobamate was first synthesized by Bernard John Ludwig, PhD, and Frank Milan Berger, MD, at Carter Products in May 1950. Wallace Laboratories, a subsidiary of Carter Products, bought the license and named it Miltown after the borough of Milltown in New Jersey.
Mood disorder	Mood disorder is the term designating a group of diagnoses in the Diagnostic and Statistical Manual of Mental Disorders (DSM IV TR) classification system where a disturbance in the person's mood is hypothesized to be the main underlying feature. The classification is known as mood (affective) disorders in ICD 10.
	English psychiatrist Henry Maudsley proposed an overarching category of affective disorder.
Obsessive-compulsive personality disorder	Obsessive-compulsive personality disorder is a personality disorder characterized by a pervasive pattern of preoccupation with orderliness, perfectionism, and mental and interpersonal control at the expense of flexibility, openness, and efficiency.

8. Medication for Mental Disorders

The primary symptoms of obsessive\ compulsive\ personality\ disorder can include preoccupation with remembering and paying attention to minute details and facts, following rules and regulations, compulsion to make lists and schedules, as well as rigidity/inflexibility of beliefs and/or exhibition of perfectionism that interferes with task-completion. Symptoms may cause extreme distress and interfere with a person's occupational and social functioning. According to the National Institute for Mental Health:

Most patients spend their early life avoiding symptoms and developing techniques to avoid dealing with these strenuous issues. Obsession

Some, but not all, patients with obsessive\ compulsive\ personality\ disorder show an obsessive need for cleanliness. This obsessive\ compulsive\ personality\ disorder trait is not to be confused with domestic efficiency; over-attention to related details may instead make these (and other) activities of daily living difficult to accomplish. Though obsessive behavior is in part a way to control anxiety, tension often remains. In the case of a hoarder, attention effectively to clean the home may be hindered by the amount of clutter that the hoarder resolves later to organize.

While there are superficial similarities between the list-making and obsessive aspects of Asperger's syndrome and obsessive\ compulsive\ personality\ disorder, the former is different from obsessive\ compulsive\ personality\ disorder especially regarding affective behaviors, including (but not limited to) empathy, social coping, and general social skills.

Perception of own and others' actions and beliefs tend to be polarised (i.e., 'right' or 'wrong', with little or no margin between the two) for people with this disorder. As might be expected, such rigidity places strain on interpersonal relationships, with frustration sometimes turning into anger and even violence. This is known as disinhibition. People with obsessive\ compulsive\ personality\ disorder often tend to general pessimism and/or underlying form(s) of depression. This can at times become so serious that suicide is a risk. Indeed, one study suggests that personality disorders are a significant substrate to psychiatric morbidity. They may cause more problems in functioning than a major depressive episode. Causes

Research into the familial tendency of obsessive\ compulsive\ personality\ disorder may be illuminated by DNA studies. Two studies suggest that people with a particular form of the DRD3 gene are highly likely to develop obsessive\ compulsive\ personality\ disorder and depression, particularly if they are male. Genetic concomitants, however, may lie dormant until triggered by events in the lives of those who are predisposed to obsessive\ compulsive\ personality\ disorder. These events could include trauma faced during childhood, such as physical, emotional or sexual abuse, or other types of psychological trauma. Diagnosis DSM

The Diagnostic and Statistical Manual of Mental Disorders fourth edition, (DSM IV-TR = 301.4), a widely used manual for diagnosing mental disorders, defines obsessive-compulsive personality disorder (in Axis II Cluster C) as:A pervasive pattern of preoccupation with orderliness, perfectionism, and mental and interpersonal control, at the expense of flexibility, openness, and efficiency, beginning by early adulthood and present in a variety of contexts. It is a requirement of DSM-IV that a diagnosis of any specific personality disorder also satisfies a set of general personality disorder criteria.Criticism

Since DSM IV-TR was published in 2000, some studies have found fault with its obsessive\ compulsive\ personality\ disorder coverage. A 2004 study challenged the usefulness of all but three of the criteria: perfectionism, rigidity and stubbornness, and miserliness. A study in 2007 found that obsessive\ compulsive\ personality\ disorder is etiologically distinct from avoidant and dependent personality disorders, suggesting it is incorrectly categorized as a Cluster C disorder. WHO

The World Health Organization's ICD-10 uses the term (F60.5) Anankastic personality disorder. It is characterized by at least three of the following:•feelings of excessive doubt and caution;•preoccupation with details, rules, lists, order, organization or schedule;•perfectionism that interferes with task completion;•excessive conscientiousness, scrupulousness, and undue preoccupation with productivity to the exclusion of pleasure and interpersonal relationships;•excessive pedantry and adherence to social conventions;•rigidity and stubbornness;•unreasonable insistence by the individual that others submit exactly to his or her way of doing things, or unreasonable reluctance to allow others to do things;•intrusion of insistent and unwelcome thoughts or impulses.Includes: •compulsive and obsessional personality (disorder)•obsessive-compulsive personality disorderExcludes: •obsessive-compulsive disorder

It is a requirement of ICD-10 that a diagnosis of any specific personality disorder also satisfies a set of general personality disorder criteria.

Panic attack	Panic attacks are periods of intense fear or apprehension that are of sudden onset and of variable duration of minutes to hours. Panic attacks usually begin abruptly, may reach a peak within 10 minutes,but may continue for much longer if the sufferer had the attack triggered by a situation from which they are not able to escape. In panic attacks that continue unabated, and are triggered by a situation from which the sufferer desires to escape, some sufferers may make frantic efforts to escape, which may be violent if others attempt to contain the sufferer.
Panic disorder	Panic disorder is an anxiety disorder characterized by recurring severe panic attacks. It may also include significant behavioral change lasting at least a month and of ongoing worry about the implications or concern about having other attacks. The latter are called anticipatory attacks (DSM-IVR).

8. Medication for Mental Disorders

Phobia	A phobia is, when used in the context of clinical psychology, a type of anxiety disorder, usually defined as a persistent fear of an object or situation in which the sufferer commits to great lengths in avoiding, typically disproportional to the actual danger posed, often being recognized as irrational. In the event the phobia cannot be avoided entirely, the sufferer will endure the situation or object with marked distress and significant interference in social or occupational activities. The terms distress and impairment as defined by the Diagnostic and Statistical Manual of Mental Disorders, Fourth Edition (DSM-IV-TR) should also take into account the context of the sufferer's environment if attempting a diagnosis.
Social influence	Social influence occurs when one's emotions, opinions, or behaviors are affected by others. Social influence takes many forms and can be seen in conformity, socialization, peer pressure, obedience, leadership, persuasion, sales, and marketing. In 1958, Harvard psychologist, Herbert Kelman identified three broad varieties of social influence.
Specific phobia	A specific phobia is a generic term for any kind of anxiety disorder that amounts to an unreasonable or irrational fear related to exposure to specific objects or situations. As a result, the affected persons tend to actively avoid direct contact with the objects or situations and, in severe cases, any mention or depiction of them. The fear or anxiety may be triggered both by the presence and the anticipation of the specific object or situation.
Lethal injection	Lethal injection is the practice of injecting a person with a fatal dose of drugs (typically a barbiturate, paralytic, and potassium solution) for the express purpose of causing the immediate death of the subject. The main application for this procedure is capital punishment, but the term may also be applied in a broad sense to euthanasia and suicide. It kills the person by first putting the person to sleep, then stopping the breathing and heart in that order.
Schizophrenia	Schizophrenia is a mental disorder characterized by a breakdown of thought processes and by poor emotional responsiveness. Common symptoms include auditory hallucinations, paranoid or bizarre delusions, or disorganized speech and thinking, and it is accompanied by significant social or occupational dysfunction. The onset of symptoms typically occurs in young adulthood, with a global lifetime prevalence of about 0.3-0.7%.
Punishment	In operant conditioning, punishment is any change in a human or animal's surroundings that occurs after a given behavior or response which reduces the likelihood of that behavior occurring again in the future. As with reinforcement, it is the behavior, not the animal, that is punished. Whether a change is or is not punishing is only known by its effect on the rate of the behavior, not by any 'hostile' or aversive features of the change.

Electroconvulsive therapy	Electroconvulsive therapy formerly known as electroshock, is a psychiatric treatment in which seizures are electrically induced in anesthetized patients for therapeutic effect. Its mode of action is unknown. Today, ECT is most often recommended for use as a treatment for severe depression that has not responded to other treatment, and is also used in the treatment of mania and catatonia.
Scientific evidence	Scientific evidence has no universally accepted definition but generally refers to evidence which serves to either support or counter a scientific theory or hypothesis. Such evidence is generally expected to be empirical and properly documented in accordance with scientific method such as is applicable to the particular field of inquiry. Standards for evidence may vary according to whether the field of inquiry is among the natural sciences or social sciences .
Tracking	Tracking is separating pupils by academic ability into groups for all subjects or certain classes and curriculum within a school. It may be referred as streaming or phasing in certain schools. In a tracking system, the entire school population is assigned to classes according to whether the students' overall achievement is above average, normal, or below average.
Chlorpromazine	Chlorpromazine is a dopamine antagonist of the typical antipsychotic class of medications possessing additional antiadrenergic, antiserotonergic, anticholinergic and antihistaminergic properties used to treat schizophrenia. First synthesized on December 11, 1950, chlorpromazine was the first drug developed with specific antipsychotic action, and would serve as the prototype for the phenothiazine class of drugs, which later grew to comprise several other agents. The introduction of chlorpromazine into clinical use has been described as the single greatest advance in psychiatric care, dramatically improving the prognosis of patients in psychiatric hospitals worldwide; the availability of antipsychotic drugs curtailed indiscriminate use of electroconvulsive therapy and psychosurgery, and was one of the driving forces behind the deinstitutionalization movement.
Mechanism	The term Social mechanisms and mechanism-based explanations of social phenomenon originate from the philosophy of science. The core idea behind the mechanism approach has been expressed as follows by Elster (1989: 3-4): 'To explain an event is to give an account of why it happened. Usually... this takes the form of citing an earlier event as the cause of the event we want to explain....
Outcome	In game theory, an outcome is a set of moves or strategies taken by the players, or it is their payoffs resulting from the actions or strategies taken by all players. The two are complementary in that, given knowledge of the set of strategies of all players, the final state of the game is known, as are any relevant payoffs. In a game where chance or a random event is involved, the outcome is not known from only the set of strategies, but is only realized when the random event(s) are realized.

8. Medication for Mental Disorders

Phenothiazine	Phenothiazine is an organic compound that occurs in various antipsychotic and antihistaminic drugs. It has the formula $S(C_6H_4)_2NH$. This yellow tricyclic compound is soluble in acetic acid, benzene, and ether. The compound is related to the thiazine-class of heterocyclic compounds.
Refusal skills	Refusal skills are a set of skills designed to help children avoid participating in high-risk behaviors. Programs designed to discourage crime, drug use, violence, and/or sexual activity frequently include refusal skills in their curricula to help students resist peer pressure while maintaining self-respect. One such program is Drug Abuse Resistance Education.
Blocking	In the statistical theory of the design of experiments, blocking is the arranging of experimental units in groups (blocks) that are similar to one another. For example, an experiment is designed to test a new drug on patients. There are two levels of the treatment, drug, and placebo, administered to male and female patients in a double blind trial.
Production	In economics, production is the act of creating output, a good or service which has value and contributes to the utility of individuals. The act may or may not include factors of production other than labor. Any effort directed toward the realization of a desired product or service is a 'productive' effort and the performance of such act is production.
Side Effects	Side Effects is a fun romantic comedy about the pharmaceutical industry starring Katherine Heigl as Karly Hert, a pharmaceutical 'detailer', who becomes disillusioned with the lack of ethics in the pharmaceutical industry and has tough choices to make. Also starring Lucian McAfee, Dorian DeMichele, Dave Durbin, Temeceka Harris. The movie's title is a reference to the medical term side effects.
Intervention	In law, intervention is a procedure to allow a nonparty, called intervenor (also spelled intervener) to join ongoing litigation, either as a matter of right or at the discretion of the court, without the permission of the original litigants. The basic rationale for intervention is that a judgment in a particular case may affect the rights of nonparties, who ideally should have the right to be heard. Intervenors are most common in appellate proceedings, but can also appear at other types of legal proceeding such as a trial.
Agent	In economics, an agent is an actor and decision maker in a model. Typically, every agent makes decisions by solving a well or ill defined optimization/choice problem. The term agent can also be seen as equivalent to player in game theory.
Amphetamine	Amphetamine or amfetamine (INN) is a psychostimulant drug of the phenethylamine class which produces increased wakefulness and focus in association with decreased fatigue and appetite. Brand names of medications that contain, or metabolize into, amphetamine include Adderall, Dexedrine, Dextrostat, Desoxyn, ProCentra, and Vyvanse, as well as Benzedrine in the past.

Diabetes	Diabetes mellitus, or simply diabetes, is a group of metabolic diseases in which a person has high blood sugar, either because the pancreas does not produce enough insulin, or because cells do not respond to the insulin that is produced. This high blood sugar produces the classical symptoms of polyuria (frequent urination), polydipsia (increased thirst) and polyphagia (increased hunger). There are three main types of diabetes mellitus (DM):•Type 1 DM results from the body's failure to produce insulin, and presently requires the person to inject insulin or wear an insulin pump.
Representation	Representation is the use of signs that stand in for and take the place of something else. It is through representation that people organize the world and reality through the act of naming its elements. Signs are arranged in order to form semantic constructions and express relations.
Survivors guilt	Survivor, survivor's, or survivors guilt is a mental condition that occurs when a person perceives themselves to have done wrong by surviving a traumatic event when others did not. It may be found among survivors of combat, natural disasters, epidemics, among the friends and family of those who have committed suicide, and in non-mortal situations such as among those whose colleagues are laid off. The experience and manifestation of survivor's guilt will depend on an individual's psychological profile.
Monitoring	In medicine, monitoring is the evaluation of a disease or condition over time. It can be performed by continuously measuring certain parameters (for example, by continuously measuring vital signs by a bedside monitor), and/or by repeatedly performing medical tests (such as blood glucose monitoring in people with diabetes mellitus). Transmitting data from a monitor to a distant monitoring station is known as telemetry or biotelemetry.
Monoamine oxidase	L-Monoamine oxidases (MAO) (EC 1.4.3.4) are a family of enzymes that catalyze the oxidation of monoamines. They are found bound to the outer membrane of mitochondria in most cell types in the body. The enzyme was originally discovered by Mary Bernheim (maiden name: Hare) in the liver and was named tyramine oxidase.
Categories	On May 14, 1867, the 27-year-old Charles Sanders Peirce, who eventually founded Pragmatism, presented a paper entitled 'On a New List of Categories' to the American Academy of Arts and Sciences. Among other things, this paper outlined a theory of predication involving three universal categories that Peirce continued to apply in philosophy and elsewhere for the rest of his life. In the categories one will discern, concentrated, the pattern which one finds formed by the three grades of clearness in 'How to Make Our Ideas Clear' (1878 foundational paper for pragmatism), and in numerous other three-way distinctions in his work.

8. Medication for Mental Disorders

Drug possession	Drug possession is the crime of having one or more illegal drugs in one's possession, either for personal use, distribution, sale or otherwise. Illegal drugs fall into different categories and sentences vary depending on the amount, type of drug, circumstances, and jurisdiction. A person has possession of drugs if he or she has actual physical control of the drugs (they have the drugs in their hands) or if the drugs are on that person.
Binge drinking	Binge drinking is the modern epithet for drinking alcoholic beverages with the primary intention of becoming intoxicated by heavy consumption of alcohol over a short period of time. It is a kind of purposeful drinking style that is popular in several countries worldwide, and overlaps somewhat with social drinking since it is often done in groups. The degree of intoxication, however, varies between and within various cultures that engage in this practice.
Liberation	Liberation is a bronze Holocaust memorial created by the sculptor Nathan Rapoport, located in New Jersey's Liberty State Park. Officially dedicated on May 30, 1985, the monument portrays an American soldier, carrying the body of a Holocaust survivor out of a Nazi concentration camp. This memorial sculpture was commissioned by the State of New Jersey and sponsored by a coalition of veterans organizations.

1. _____ is the crime of having one or more illegal drugs in one's possession, either for personal use, distribution, sale or otherwise. Illegal drugs fall into different categories and sentences vary depending on the amount, type of drug, circumstances, and jurisdiction. A person has possession of drugs if he or she has actual physical control of the drugs (they have the drugs in their hands) or if the drugs are on that person.

   a. Failure to appear
   b. Failure to obey a police order
   c. Drug possession
   d. Fence

2. . _____ is a national social insurance program, administered by the U.S. federal government in 1965, that guarantees access to health insurance for Americans ages 65 and older and younger people with disabilities as well as people with end stage renal disease. As a social insurance program, _____ spreads the financial risk associated with illness across society to protect everyone, and thus has a somewhat different social role from private insurers, which must manage their risk portfolio to guarantee their own solvency.

   _____ offers all enrollees a defined benefit.

    a. Mutual exchange
    b. Medicare
    c. Parental leave
    d. Severe Disablement Allowance

3. _____ is one hypothesis about the cause of mental illness. Other causes that are debated include psychological and social causes.

The basic concept is that neurotransmitter imbalances within the brain are the main causes of psychiatric conditions and that these conditions can be improved with medication which corrects these imbalances.

    a. Psychoneuroendocrinology
    b. Chemical imbalance
    c. Edinburgh Postnatal Depression Scale
    d. Emotional detachment

4. A _____ or mental illness is a psychological pattern or anomaly, potentially reflected in behavior, that is generally associated with distress or disability, and which is not considered part of normal development of a person's culture. _____s are generally defined by a combination of how a person feels, acts, thinks or perceives. This may be associated with particular regions or functions of the brain or rest of the nervous system, often in a social context.

    a. Mental disorder
    b. Visa overstay
    c. withdrawl
    d. Severe Disablement Allowance

5. In economics, _____ is the act of creating output, a good or service which has value and contributes to the utility of individuals. The act may or may not include factors of _____ other than labor. Any effort directed toward the realization of a desired product or service is a 'productive' effort and the performance of such act is _____.

    a. Production
    b. Rule of three
    c. Term
    d. VPIN

1. c
2. b
3. b
4. a
5. a

You can take the complete Chapter Practice Test

for 8. Medication for Mental Disorders
on all key terms, persons, places, and concepts.

Online 99 Cents

http://www.epub4.1.22005.8.cram101.com/

Use www.Cram101.com for all your study needs

including Cram101's online interactive problem solving labs in

chemistry, statistics, mathematics, and more.

9. Alcohol

CHAPTER OUTLINE: KEY TERMS, PEOPLE, PLACES, CONCEPTS

_____	Ethanol
_____	Sigmund Freud
_____	Substance abuse
_____	Western world
_____	Frontal lobe
_____	Production
_____	Mickey Finn
_____	Controlled substance
_____	Efficacy
_____	Grief
_____	Confession
_____	Meprobamate
_____	Outcome
_____	Autonomous language
_____	Adderall
_____	Cocaine
_____	Temperance
_____	National park
_____	Amendments
_____	Patent medicine
_____	Great Depression

	Hip flask
	Speakeasy
	Strengthening Families
	Norm
	Binge drinking
	Absorption
	Distribution
	Liver
	Diabetes
	Intake
	Alcohol dependence
	Euphoria
	Codeine
	Medical amnesty policy
	Nursing home
	Reduction
	Seriousness
	Time-out
	Screening
	Sexual assault
	Arousal

Blackout

Drug user

Homicide

Suicide Tuesday

Dilation

Mechanism

Suicide

Hangover

Immune system

Abortion

Spontaneous abortion

Data set

Survivors guilt

Benzedrine

Administration

Inheritance

Ethanol	Ethanol, pure alcohol, grain alcohol, or drinking alcohol, is a volatile, flammable, colorless liquid. It is a powerful psychoactive drug and one of the oldest recreational drugs. Best known as the type of alcohol found in alcoholic beverages, it is also used in thermometers, as a solvent, and as an alcohol fuel.
Sigmund Freud	Sigmund Freud was an Austrian neurologist who became known as the founding father of psychoanalysis. Freud's parents were poor, but they ensured his education. Freud chose medicine as a career and qualified as a doctor at the University of Vienna, subsequently undertaking research into cerebral palsy, aphasia and microscopic neuroanatomy at the Vienna General Hospital.
Substance abuse	Substance abuse, also known as drug abuse, is a patterned use of a substance (drug) in which the user consumes the substance in amounts or with methods neither approved nor supervised by medical professionals. Substance abuse/drug abuse is not limited to mood-altering or psycho-active drugs. If an activity is performed using the objects against the rules and policies of the matter (as in steroids for performance enhancement in sports), it is also called substance abuse.
Western world	The Western world, is a term referring to different nations depending on the context. There is no agreed upon definition about what all these nations have in common apart from having a significant population of European descent and having cultures and societies heavily influenced by and connected to Europe. The concept of the Western part of the earth has its roots in Greco-Roman civilization in Europe, with the advent of Christianity.
Frontal lobe	The frontal lobe is an area in the brain of humans and other mammals, located at the front of each cerebral hemisphere and positioned anterior to (in front of) the parietal lobe and superior and anterior to the temporal lobes. It is separated from the parietal lobe by a space between tissues called the central sulcus, and from the temporal lobe by a deep fold called the lateral (Sylvian) sulcus. The post-central gyrus, forming the posterior border of the frontal lobe, contains the primary motor cortex, which controls voluntary movements of specific body parts.
Production	In economics, production is the act of creating output, a good or service which has value and contributes to the utility of individuals. The act may or may not include factors of production other than labor. Any effort directed toward the realization of a desired product or service is a 'productive' effort and the performance of such act is production.
Mickey Finn	A Mickey Finn is a slang term for a drink laced with a drug (especially chloral hydrate) given to someone without their knowledge in order to incapacitate them. Serving someone a Mickey Finn is most commonly referred to as slipping a mickey, sometimes spelled 'slipping a mickie'.

9. Alcohol

	History of term
	The Chicago bartender Michael 'Mickey' Finn
	The Mickey Finn is most likely named for the manager and bartender of a Chicago establishment, the Lone Star Saloon and Palm Garden Restaurant, which operated from 1896 to 1903 in the city's South Loop neighborhood on South State Street.
Controlled substance	A controlled substance is generally a drug or chemical whose manufacture, possession, and use are regulated by a government. This may include illegal drugs and prescription medications (designated Controlled Drug in the United Kingdom).
Efficacy	Efficacy is the capacity to produce an effect. It has different specific meanings in different fields. In medicine, it is the ability of an intervention or drug to reproduce a desired effect in expert hands and under ideal circumstances.
Grief	Grief is a multi-faceted response to loss, particularly to the loss of someone or something to which a bond was formed. Although conventionally focused on the emotional response to loss, it also has physical, cognitive, behavioral, social, and philosophical dimensions. While the terms are often used interchangeably, bereavement refers to the state of loss, and grief is the reaction to loss.
Confession	In the law of criminal evidence, a confession is a statement by a suspect in crime which is adverse to that person. Some authorities, such as Black's Law Dictionary, define a confession in more narrow terms, e.g. as 'a statement admitting or acknowledging all facts necessary for conviction of a crime,' which would be distinct from a mere admission of certain facts that, if true, would still not, by themselves, satisfy all the elements of the offense.
	This specific form of testimony, involving oneself, is used as a form of proof in judicial matters, since at least the Inquisition.
Meprobamate	Meprobamate is a carbamate derivative which is used as an anxiolytic drug. It was the best-selling minor tranquilizer for a time, but has largely been replaced by the benzodiazepines.
	History
	Meprobamate was first synthesized by Bernard John Ludwig, PhD, and Frank Milan Berger, MD, at Carter Products in May 1950. Wallace Laboratories, a subsidiary of Carter Products, bought the license and named it Miltown after the borough of Milltown in New Jersey.
Outcome	In game theory, an outcome is a set of moves or strategies taken by the players, or it is their payoffs resulting from the actions or strategies taken by all players.

The two are complementary in that, given knowledge of the set of strategies of all players, the final state of the game is known, as are any relevant payoffs. In a game where chance or a random event is involved, the outcome is not known from only the set of strategies, but is only realized when the random event(s) are realized.

Autonomous language	An autonomous language is usually a standard language that has its own established norms, as opposed to a heteronomous variety.
	An autonomous language will usually have grammar books, dictionaries and literature written in it. Autonomy is largely a sociopolitical construct rather than a result of specific linguistic differences.
Adderall	Adderall is a brand-name psychostimulant medication composed of racemic amphetamine aspartate monohydrate, racemic amphetamine sulfate, dextroamphetamine saccharide, and dextroamphetamine sulfate, which is thought by scientists to work by increasing the amount of dopamine and norepinephrine in the brain. In addition, the drug also acts as a potent dopamine reuptake inhibitor and norepinephrine reuptake inhibitor. Adderall is widely reported to increase alertness, increase libido, increase concentration and overall cognitive performance, and, in general, improve mood, while decreasing user fatigue.
Cocaine	Cocaine is a 1922 British crime film directed by Graham Cutts and starring Hilda Bayley, Flora Le Breton, Ward McAllister and Cyril Raymond. A melodrama - it depicts the distribution of cocaine by gangsters through a series of London nightclubs and the revenge sought by a man after the death of his daughter.
	Because of its depiction of drug use, it was the most controversial British film of the 1920s.
Temperance	Temperance has been studied by religious thinkers, philosophers, and more recently, psychologists, particularly in the positive psychology movement. It is considered a virtue, a core value that can be seen consistently across time and cultures . It is considered one of the four cardinal virtues, for it is believed that no virtue could be sustained in the face of inability to control oneself, if the virtue was opposed to some desire.
National park	A national park is a reserve of natural or semi-natural land, declared or owned by a government, set aside for human recreation and enjoyment, animal and environmental protection and restricted from most development. While ideas for national parks had been suggested previously, the first one established, in 1872, was the United States' Yellowstone National Park. An international organization, the International Union for Conservation of Nature (IUCN), and its World Commission on Protected Areas, has defined National Parks as its category II type of protected areas.
Amendments	A constitutional amendment is a formal change to the text of the written constitution of a nation or state. In some jurisdictions the text of the constitution itself is altered; in others the text is not changed, but the amendments change its effect.

9. Alcohol

Patent medicine	Patent medicine refers to medical compounds of questionable effectiveness sold under a variety of names and labels. The term 'patent medicine' is somewhat of a misnomer because, in most cases, although many of the products were trademarked, they were never patented (most avoided the patent process so as not to reveal products' often hazardous and questionable ingredients). Perhaps the only 'patent medicine' ever to be patented was Castoria.
Great Depression	The Great Depression was a severe worldwide economic depression in the decade preceding World War II. The timing of the Great Depression varied across nations, but in most countries it started in about 1929 and lasted until the late 1930s or early 1940s. It was the longest, most widespread, and deepest depression of the 20th century. In the 21st century, the Great Depression is commonly used as an example of how far the world's economy can decline.
Hip flask	A hip flask is a thin flask for holding a distilled beverage; its size and shape are suited to a trouser pocket. Hip flasks were traditionally made of pewter, silver, or even glass, though most modern flasks are made from stainless steel. Some modern flasks are made of plastic so as to avoid detection by metal detectors.
Speakeasy	Speakeasy is a numerical computing interactive environment also featuring an interpreted programming language. It was initially developed for internal use at the Physics Division of Argonne National Laboratory by the theoretical physicist Stanley Cohen. He eventually founded Speakeasy Computing Corporation to make the program available commercially.
Strengthening Families	Strengthening Families is an approach to working with children and families to build 'Protective Factors' that can prevent child abuse and child neglect. The approach is being implemented in early care and education centers, child welfare departments, and other venues across the United States. Strengthening Families is a project of the Center for the Study of Social Policy.
Norm	Social norms are the behaviors and cues within a society or group. This sociological term has been defined as 'the rules that a group uses for appropriate and inappropriate values, beliefs, attitudes and behaviors. These rules may be explicit or implicit.
Binge drinking	Binge drinking is the modern epithet for drinking alcoholic beverages with the primary intention of becoming intoxicated by heavy consumption of alcohol over a short period of time. It is a kind of purposeful drinking style that is popular in several countries worldwide, and overlaps somewhat with social drinking since it is often done in groups. The degree of intoxication, however, varies between and within various cultures that engage in this practice.

Absorption	In economics, absorption is the total demand for all final marketed goods and services by all economic agents resident in an economy, regardless of the origin of the goods and services themselves. As the absorption is equal to the sum of all domestically-produced goods consumed locally and all imports, it is equal to national income [Y = C + I + G + (X - M)] minus the balance of trade [X - M]. The term was coined, and its relation to the balance of trade identified, by Sidney Alexander in 1952.
Distribution	Distribution in economics refers to the way total output, income, or wealth is distributed among individuals or among the factors of production (such as labour, land, and capital).. In general theory and the national income and product accounts, each unit of output corresponds to a unit of income. One use of national accounts is for classifying factor incomes and measuring their respective shares, as in National Income.
Liver	The liver, hepar, is a vital organ present in vertebrates and some other animals. It has a wide range of functions, including detoxification, protein synthesis, and production of biochemicals necessary for digestion. The liver is necessary for survival; there is currently no way to compensate for the absence of liver function in the long term, although new liver dialysis techniques can be used in the short term.
Diabetes	Diabetes mellitus, or simply diabetes, is a group of metabolic diseases in which a person has high blood sugar, either because the pancreas does not produce enough insulin, or because cells do not respond to the insulin that is produced. This high blood sugar produces the classical symptoms of polyuria (frequent urination), polydipsia (increased thirst) and polyphagia (increased hunger). There are three main types of diabetes mellitus (DM):•Type 1 DM results from the body's failure to produce insulin, and presently requires the person to inject insulin or wear an insulin pump.
Intake	An intake is a parcel of land, of the order of 12 hectares (30 acres), which has been 'taken in' from a moor and brought under cultivation. The term is used almost exclusively in the north of England applying to land on the fringes of the Pennines and other moors. The creation of intakes went on from medieval times up to the 19th century.
Alcohol dependence	Alcohol dependence is a psychiatric diagnosis (a substance related disorder DSM-IV) describing an entity in which an individual uses alcohol despite significant areas of dysfunction, evidence of physical dependence, and/or related hardship, and also may cause stress and bipolar disorder.

9. Alcohol

CHAPTER HIGHLIGHTS & NOTES: KEY TERMS, PEOPLE, PLACES, CONCEPTS

According to the DSM-IV criteria for alcohol dependence, at least three out of seven of the following criteria must be manifest during a 12 month period:•Tolerance•Withdrawal symptoms or clinically defined Alcohol Withdrawal Syndrome•Use in larger amounts or for longer periods than intended•Persistent desire or unsuccessful efforts to cut down on alcohol use•Time is spent obtaining alcohol or recovering from effects•Social, occupational and recreational pursuits are given up or reduced because of alcohol use•Use is continued despite knowledge of alcohol-related harm (physical or psychological)History and epidemiology

About 12% of American adults have had an alcohol dependence problem at some time in their life. The term 'alcohol dependence' has replaced 'alcoholism' as a term in order that individuals do not internalize the idea of cure and disease, but can approach alcohol as a chemical they may depend upon to cope with outside pressures.

Euphoria	Euphoria is medically recognized as a mental and emotional condition in which a person experiences intense feelings of well-being, elation, happiness, ecstasy, excitement and joy. Technically, euphoria is an affect, but the term is often colloquially used to define emotion as an intense state of transcendent happiness combined with an overwhelming sense of contentment. It has also been defined as an 'affective state of exaggerated well-being or elation.' The word derives from Greek ε?φορ?α, 'power of enduring easily, fertility'.
Codeine	Codeine or 3-methylmorphine (a natural isomer of methylated morphine, the other being the semi-synthetic 6-methylmorphine) is an opiate used for its analgesic, antitussive, and antidiarrheal properties. Codeine is the second-most predominant alkaloid in opium, at up to 3 percent; it is much more prevalent in the Iranian poppy (Papaver bractreatum), and codeine is extracted from this species in some places although the below-mentioned morphine methylation process is still much more common. It is considered the prototype of the weak to midrange opioids.
Medical amnesty policy	Medical Amnesty Policies are laws or acts enacted protecting from liability those who seek medical attention as a result of illegal actions. Such policies have been developing most notably in colleges in the United States regarding alcohol and drug use by students. Schools such as Cornell University have implemented such policies to protect students seeking medical attention from legal action for underage drinking and possession of alcohol and/or drugs. The purpose of such policies is to reduce the hesitation caused by fear of legal action to seek medical attention. Similar policies are applicable at many levels: Colleges and universities, local communities, as well as state governments and the federal government. Medical amnesty policies were first present in the University setting. Although failure to seek medical assistance in cases of alcohol poisoning can lead to fatal outcomes, evidence suggests that the threat of judicial consequences resulting from enforcement of the minimum drinking age or other law or policy violations leads some students to refrain from calling for emergency medical services.

Visit Cram101.com for full Practice Exams

Nursing home	A nursing home, convalescent home, Skilled Nursing Unit (SNU), care home or rest home provides a type of care of residents: it is a place of residence for people who require constant nursing care and have significant deficiencies with activities of daily living. Residents include the elderly and younger adults with physical or mental disabilities. Residents in a skilled nursing facility may also receive physical, occupational, and other rehabilitative therapies following an accident or illness.
Reduction	In philosophy, reduction is the process by which one object, property, concept, theory, etc., is shown to be explicable in terms of another, lower level, entity. For example, we say that physical properties such as the boiling point of a substance are reducible to that substance's molecular properties, because statistical mechanics explain why a liquid boils at a certain temperature using only the properties of its constituent atoms. Thus we might also describe reduction as a process analogous to absorption, by which one theory is wholly subsumed under another.
Seriousness	Seriousness is an attitude of gravity, solemnity, persistence, and earnestness toward something considered to be of importance. Some notable philosophers and commentators have criticised excessive seriousness, while others have praised it. Seriousness is often contrasted with comedy, as in the seriocomedy.
Time-out	A time-out involves temporarily separating a child from an environment where inappropriate behavior has occurred, and is intended to remove positive reinforcement of the behavior. It is an educational and parenting technique recommended by some pediatricians and developmental psychologists as an effective form of child discipline. Often a corner (hence the common term corner time) or a similar space where the child is to stand or sit during time-outs is designated.
Screening	Screening in economics refers to a strategy of combating adverse selection, one of the potential decision-making complications in cases of asymmetric information. The concept of screening was first developed by Michael Spence (1973), and should be distinguished from signalling, which implies that the informed agent moves first. For purposes of screening, asymmetric information cases assume two economic agents--which we call, for example, Abel and Cain--where Abel knows more about himself than Cain knows about Abel.
Sexual assault	Sexual assault is an assault of a sexual nature on another person, or any sexual act committed without consent. Although sexual assaults most frequently are by a man on a woman, it may involve any combination of two or more men, women and children. The term sexual assault is used, in public discourse, as a generic term that is defined as any involuntary sexual act in which a person is threatened, coerced, or forced to engage against their will, or any sexual touching of a person who has not consented.

9. Alcohol

Arousal	Arousal is a physiological and psychological state of being awake or reactive to stimuli. It involves the activation of the reticular activating system in the brain stem, the autonomic nervous system and the endocrine system, leading to increased heart rate and blood pressure and a condition of sensory alertness, mobility and readiness to respond. There are many different neural systems involved in what is collectively known as the arousal system.
Blackout	A blackout is a phenomenon caused by the intake of alcohol or other substance in which long term memory creation is impaired or there is a complete inability to recall the past. Blackouts are frequently described as having effects similar to that of anterograde amnesia, in which the subject cannot create memories after the event that caused amnesia. 'Blacking out' is not to be confused with the mutually exclusive act of 'passing out', which means loss of consciousness.
Drug user	A drug user is a person who uses drugs either legally or illegally. The term user is typically employed more to refer to illegal drug use by a person who is often part of a subculture of recreational drug use. Drug users are often referred to as 'heads', depending on the drug used, i.e., pothead, hophead, crackhead, etc.
Homicide	Homicide refers to the act of a human killing another human. Murder, for example, is a type of homicide. It can also describe a person who has committed such an act, though this use is rare in modern English.
Suicide Tuesday	Suicide Tuesday is a slang term for the depressive period following the use of MDMA (ecstasy). This term is currently thought to be in use throughout the world where ecstasy is highly used. Suicide Tuesday refers to the Tuesday after MDMA use, typically on a Friday or Saturday.
Dilation	In mathematics, a dilation is a function f from a metric space into itself that satisfies the identity $d(f(x), f(y)) = r d(x, y)$ for all points (x, y) where $d(x, y)$ is the distance from x to y and r is some positive real number. In Euclidean space, such a dilation is a similarity of the space. Dilations change the size but not the shape of an object or figure.
Mechanism	The term Social mechanisms and mechanism-based explanations of social phenomenon originate from the philosophy of science.

The core idea behind the mechanism approach has been expressed as follows by Elster (1989: 3-4): 'To explain an event is to give an account of why it happened. Usually... this takes the form of citing an earlier event as the cause of the event we want to explain....

Suicide

Suicide was one of the groundbreaking books in the field of sociology. Written by French sociologist Émile Durkheim and published in 1897 it was a case study (some argue that it is not a case study, and that this is what makes it unique among other scholarly work on the same subject) of suicide, a publication unique for its time which provided an example of what the sociological monograph should look like.

Durkheim explores the differing suicide rates among Protestants and Catholics, arguing that stronger social control among Catholics results in lower suicide rates.

Hangover

A hangover is the experience of various unpleasant physiological effects following heavy consumption of alcoholic beverages. The most commonly reported characteristics of a hangover include headache, nausea, sensitivity to light and noise, lethargy, dysphoria, diarrhea and thirst, typically after the intoxicating effect of the alcohol begins to wear off. While a hangover can be experienced at any time, generally speaking a hangover is experienced the morning after a night of heavy drinking.

Immune system

The immune system is a system of biological structures and processes within an organism that protects against disease. To function properly, an immune system must detect a wide variety of agents, from viruses to parasitic worms, and distinguish them from the organism's own healthy tissue.

Pathogens can rapidly evolve and adapt, and thereby avoid detection and neutralization by the immune system, however, multiple defense mechanisms have also evolved to recognize and neutralize pathogens.

Abortion

Abortion is defined as the termination of pregnancy by the removal or expulsion from the uterus of a fetus or embryo prior to viability. An abortion can occur spontaneously, in which case it is usually called a miscarriage, or it can be purposely induced. The term abortion most commonly refers to the induced abortion of a human pregnancy.

Spontaneous abortion

Miscarriage or spontaneous abortion is the spontaneous end of a pregnancy at a stage where the embryo or fetus is incapable of surviving, generally defined in humans at prior to 20 weeks of gestation. Miscarriage is the most common complication of early pregnancy.

Terminology

9. Alcohol

Data set	A data set is a collection of data, usually presented in tabular form. Each column represents a particular variable. Each row corresponds to a given member of the data set in question.
Survivors guilt	Survivor, survivor's, or survivors guilt is a mental condition that occurs when a person perceives themselves to have done wrong by surviving a traumatic event when others did not. It may be found among survivors of combat, natural disasters, epidemics, among the friends and family of those who have committed suicide, and in non-mortal situations such as among those whose colleagues are laid off. The experience and manifestation of survivor's guilt will depend on an individual's psychological profile.
Benzedrine	Benzedrine is the trade name of the racemic mixture of amphetamine (dl-amphetamine). It was marketed under this brandname in the USA by Smith, Kline & French in the form of inhalers, starting in 1928. Benzedrine was used to enlarge nasal and bronchial passages and it is closely related to other stimulants produced later, such as dextroamphetamine (d-amphetamine) and methamphetamine. Benzedrine should not be confused with the fundamentally different substance benzphetamine.
Administration	As a legal concept, administration is a procedure under the insolvency laws of a number of common law jurisdictions. It functions as a rescue mechanism for insolvent entities and allows them to carry on running their business. The process - an alternative to liquidation - is often known as going into administration.
Inheritance	Inheritance is the practice of passing on property, titles, debts, rights and obligations upon the death of an individual. It represents also to pass a characteristic, genetically. It has long played an important role in human societies.

1. As a legal concept, _____ is a procedure under the insolvency laws of a number of common law jurisdictions. It functions as a rescue mechanism for insolvent entities and allows them to carry on running their business. The process - an alternative to liquidation - is often known as going into _____.

    a. Administration
    b. Examinership
    c. Order to show cause
    d. King effect

2. . _____ or 3-methylmorphine (a natural isomer of methylated morphine, the other being the semi-synthetic 6-methylmorphine) is an opiate used for its analgesic, antitussive, and antidiarrheal properties.

_____ is the second-most predominant alkaloid in opium, at up to 3 percent; it is much more prevalent in the Iranian poppy (Papaver bractreatum), and _____ is extracted from this species in some places although the below-mentioned morphine methylation process is still much more common. It is considered the prototype of the weak to midrange opioids.

a. Co-codamol
b. Co-codaprin
c. Codeine
d. Hodgkinsine

3. _____, also known as drug abuse, is a patterned use of a substance (drug) in which the user consumes the substance in amounts or with methods neither approved nor supervised by medical professionals. _____/drug abuse is not limited to mood-altering or psycho-active drugs. If an activity is performed using the objects against the rules and policies of the matter (as in steroids for performance enhancement in sports), it is also called _____.

a. Substance abuse
b. cerebral palsy
c. Down syndrome
d. Passive-aggressive

4. _____ is a physiological and psychological state of being awake or reactive to stimuli. It involves the activation of the reticular activating system in the brain stem, the autonomic nervous system and the endocrine system, leading to increased heart rate and blood pressure and a condition of sensory alertness, mobility and readiness to respond.

There are many different neural systems involved in what is collectively known as the _____ system.

a. Awesome Face
b. Ecstasy
c. Embarrassment
d. Arousal

5. The _____, hepar, is a vital organ present in vertebrates and some other animals. It has a wide range of functions, including detoxification, protein synthesis, and production of biochemicals necessary for digestion. The _____ is necessary for survival; there is currently no way to compensate for the absence of _____ function in the long term, although new _____ dialysis techniques can be used in the short term.

a. Visa overstay
b. Liver
c. Gender pay gap
d. Gender pay gap in Australia

1. a
2. c
3. a
4. d
5. b

You can take the complete Chapter Practice Test

for 9. Alcohol
on all key terms, persons, places, and concepts.

Online 99 Cents

http://www.epub4.1.22005.9.cram101.com/

Use www.Cram101.com for all your study needs

including Cram101's online interactive problem solving labs in

chemistry, statistics, mathematics, and more.

10. Tobacco

Discovery

Monopoly

Product placement

Incidence

Lawsuit

Lung

Warning

Monitoring

Cocaine dependence

Side Effects

Higher Ground

Abortion

Birth weight

Reduction

Spontaneous abortion

Exposure

Absorption

Administration

Emperor

Smuggling

Discovery	Discovery is the act of detecting something new, or something 'old' that had been unknown. With reference to science and academic disciplines, discovery is the observation of new phenomena, new actions, or new events and providing new reasoning to explain the knowledge gathered through such observations with previously acquired knowledge from abstract thought and everyday experiences. Visual discoveries are often called sightings.
Monopoly	Monopoly is a board game published by Parker Brothers. he economic concept of monopoly, the domination of a market by a single entity. The history of Monopoly can be traced back to 1904, when an American woman named Elizabeth (Lizzie) J. Magie Phillips created a game through which she hoped to be able to explain the single tax theory of Henry George (it was intended to illustrate the negative aspects of concentrating land in private monopolies).
Product placement	Product placement, is a form of advertisement, where branded goods or services are placed in a context usually devoid of ads, such as movies, music videos, the story line of television shows, or news programs. The product placement is often not disclosed at the time that the good or service is featured. Product placement became common in the 1990s, until the ramifications of product placement were clearly understood.
Incidence	Incidence is a measure of the risk of developing some new condition within a specified period of time. Although sometimes loosely expressed simply as the number of new cases during some time period, it is better expressed as a proportion or a rate with a denominator. Incidence proportion (also known as cumulative incidence) is the number of new cases within a specified time period divided by the size of the population initially at risk.
Lawsuit	A lawsuit is a civil action brought in a court of law in which a plaintiff, a party who claims to have incurred loss as a result of a defendant's actions, demands a legal or equitable remedy. The defendant is required to respond to the plaintiff's complaint. If the plaintiff is successful, judgment will be given in the plaintiff's favor, and a variety of court orders may be issued to enforce a right, award damages, or impose a temporary or permanent injunction to prevent an act or compel an act.
Lung	Lung (Tibetan: rlung) is a word that means wind or breath. It is a key concept in the Vajrayana traditions of Tibetan Buddhism and has a variety of meanings. Lung is a concept that's particularly important to understandings of the subtle body and the Three Vajras (body, speech and mind).
Warning	When a traffic stop is made, a warning issued by the officer is a statement that the motorist has committed some offense, but is being spared the actual citation. Officers can use their own discretion whether to issue a citation or warning.

10. Tobacco

Monitoring	In medicine, monitoring is the evaluation of a disease or condition over time.
	It can be performed by continuously measuring certain parameters (for example, by continuously measuring vital signs by a bedside monitor), and/or by repeatedly performing medical tests (such as blood glucose monitoring in people with diabetes mellitus).
	Transmitting data from a monitor to a distant monitoring station is known as telemetry or biotelemetry.
Cocaine dependence	Cocaine dependence is a psychological desire to regularly use cocaine. It can result in cardiovascular and brain damage such as constricting blood vessels in the brain, causing strokes and constricting arteries in the heart, causing heart attacks specifically in the central nervous system.
	The use of cocaine can cause mood swings, paranoia, insomnia, psychosis, high blood pressure, tachycardia, panic attacks, cognitive impairments and drastic changes in the personality that can lead to aggressive, compulsive, criminal and/or erratic behaviors.
Side Effects	Side Effects is a fun romantic comedy about the pharmaceutical industry starring Katherine Heigl as Karly Hert, a pharmaceutical 'detailer', who becomes disillusioned with the lack of ethics in the pharmaceutical industry and has tough choices to make. Also starring Lucian McAfee, Dorian DeMichele, Dave Durbin, Temeceka Harris. The movie's title is a reference to the medical term side effects.
Higher Ground	Higher Ground is a 501(C)3 HIV-AIDS non-profit support group based in Royal Oak, Michigan. Founded in 2002, it primarily serves metropolitan Detroit and southeastern Michigan. It frequently receives media coverage for public service.
Abortion	Abortion is defined as the termination of pregnancy by the removal or expulsion from the uterus of a fetus or embryo prior to viability. An abortion can occur spontaneously, in which case it is usually called a miscarriage, or it can be purposely induced. The term abortion most commonly refers to the induced abortion of a human pregnancy.
Birth weight	Birth weight is the body weight of a baby at its birth.
	There have been numerous studies that have attempted, with varying degrees of success, to show links between birth weight and later-life conditions, including diabetes, obesity, tobacco smoking and intelligence. Determinants
	There are basically two distinct determinants for birth weight:•The duration of gestation prior to birth, that is, the gestational age at which the child is born•The prenatal growth rate, generally measured in relation to what weight is expected for any gestational age.

The incidence of birth weight being outside what is normal is influenced by the parents in numerous ways, including:•Genetics•The health of the mother, particularly during the pregnancy•Environmental factors, including exposure of the mother to secondhand smoke•Economic status of the parents gives inconsistent study findings according to a review on 2010, and remains speculative as a determinant.•Other factors, like multiple births, where each baby is likely to be outside the AGA, one more so than the otherAbnormalities •A low birth weight can be caused either by a preterm birth (low gestational age at birth) or of the infant being small for gestational age (slow prenatal growth rate), or a combination of both.•A very large birth weight is usually caused by the infant having been large for gestational ageInfluence on adult life

Studies have been conducted to investigate how a person's birth weight can influence aspects of their future life.

Reduction	In philosophy, reduction is the process by which one object, property, concept, theory, etc., is shown to be explicable in terms of another, lower level, entity. For example, we say that physical properties such as the boiling point of a substance are reducible to that substance's molecular properties, because statistical mechanics explain why a liquid boils at a certain temperature using only the properties of its constituent atoms. Thus we might also describe reduction as a process analogous to absorption, by which one theory is wholly subsumed under another.
Spontaneous abortion	Miscarriage or spontaneous abortion is the spontaneous end of a pregnancy at a stage where the embryo or fetus is incapable of surviving, generally defined in humans at prior to 20 weeks of gestation. Miscarriage is the most common complication of early pregnancy. Terminology Very early miscarriages--those that occur before the sixth week LMP (since the woman's Last Menstrual Period)--are medically termed early pregnancy loss or chemical pregnancy.
Exposure	Exposure in magic refers to the practice of revealing the secrets of how magic tricks are performed. The practice is generally frowned upon as a type of spoiler that ruins the experience of magical performances for audiences. Background Exposures are performed by both professional and amateur magicians.
Absorption	In economics, absorption is the total demand for all final marketed goods and services by all economic agents resident in an economy, regardless of the origin of the goods and services themselves. As the absorption is equal to the sum of all domestically-produced goods consumed locally and all imports, it is equal to national income $[Y = C + I + G + (X - M)]$ minus the balance of trade $[X - M]$.

10. Tobacco

Administration	As a legal concept, administration is a procedure under the insolvency laws of a number of common law jurisdictions. It functions as a rescue mechanism for insolvent entities and allows them to carry on running their business. The process - an alternative to liquidation - is often known as going into administration.
Emperor	An emperor is a (male) monarch, usually the sovereign ruler of an empire or another type of imperial realm. Empress, the female equivalent, may indicate an emperor's wife (empress consort) or a woman who rules in her own right (empress regnant). Emperors are generally recognized to be of a higher honor and rank than kings.
Smuggling	Smuggling is the clandestine transportation of goods or persons, such as out of a building, into a prison, or across an international border, in violation of applicable laws or other regulations. There are various motivations to smuggle. These include the participation in illegal trade, such as in the drug trade, in illegal immigration or illegal emigration, tax evasion, providing contraband to a prison inmate, or the theft of the items being smuggled.

1. _____ (Tibetan: r_____) is a word that means wind or breath. It is a key concept in the Vajrayana traditions of Tibetan Buddhism and has a variety of meanings. _____ is a concept that's particularly important to understandings of the subtle body and the Three Vajras (body, speech and mind).

   a. Naturopathy
   b. Numen
   c. Lung
   d. Prana

2. _____ is a 501(C)3 HIV-AIDS non-profit support group based in Royal Oak, Michigan. Founded in 2002, it primarily serves metropolitan Detroit and southeastern Michigan. It frequently receives media coverage for public service.

   a. Hipster PDA
   b. Hoffman Institute
   c. Holland Codes
   d. Higher Ground

3. . _____ in magic refers to the practice of revealing the secrets of how magic tricks are performed.

   The practice is generally frowned upon as a type of spoiler that ruins the experience of magical performances for audiences.

Background

_____s are performed by both professional and amateur magicians.

a. Illegal number
b. Inevitable disclosure
c. Old Bay Seasoning
d. Exposure

4. _____ is a board game published by Parker Brothers. he economic concept of _____, the domination of a market by a single entity.

The history of _____ can be traced back to 1904, when an American woman named Elizabeth (Lizzie) J. Magie Phillips created a game through which she hoped to be able to explain the single tax theory of Henry George (it was intended to illustrate the negative aspects of concentrating land in private _____(ies)).

a. Monopoly money
b. Monopoly
c. Mytopia
d. Pardus

5. _____ is the act of detecting something new, or something 'old' that had been unknown. With reference to science and academic disciplines, _____ is the observation of new phenomena, new actions, or new events and providing new reasoning to explain the knowledge gathered through such observations with previously acquired knowledge from abstract thought and everyday experiences. Visual _____(ies) are often called sightings.

a. Discrimination learning
b. Dreyfus model of skill acquisition
c. Discovery
d. Habituation

1. c

2. d

3. d

4. b

5. c

You can take the complete Chapter Practice Test

for 10. Tobacco
on all key terms, persons, places, and concepts.

Online 99 Cents

http://www.epub4.1.22005.10.cram101.com/

Use www.Cram101.com for all your study needs

including Cram101's online interactive problem solving labs in

chemistry, statistics, mathematics, and more.

11. Caffeine

	Coffeehouse
	Revenue
	Representation
	Distribution
	Higher Ground
	Tea bag
	Social influence
	Psilocybin
	Substance abuse
	Stimulation
	Mickey Finn
	Panic attack
	Risk factor
	Alcohol dependence
	Autonomous language

Coffeehouse	A coffeehouse is a social event, often held to raise funds for and/or generate awareness of a social cause or other event.
	The name 'coffeehouse' is derived from the limited menu which is typically available at the social event: coffee is usually the featured beverage, together with other non-alcoholic beverages such as soda, juice and tea. Desserts and snack foods may round out the menu.
Revenue	In business, revenue is income that a company receives from its normal business activities, usually from the sale of goods and services to customers. In many countries, such as the United Kingdom, revenue is referred to as turnover. Some companies receive revenue from interest, dividends or royalties paid to them by other companies.
Representation	Representation is the use of signs that stand in for and take the place of something else. It is through representation that people organize the world and reality through the act of naming its elements. Signs are arranged in order to form semantic constructions and express relations.
Distribution	Distribution in economics refers to the way total output, income, or wealth is distributed among individuals or among the factors of production (such as labour, land, and capital).. In general theory and the national income and product accounts, each unit of output corresponds to a unit of income. One use of national accounts is for classifying factor incomes and measuring their respective shares, as in National Income.
Higher Ground	Higher Ground is a 501(C)3 HIV-AIDS non-profit support group based in Royal Oak, Michigan. Founded in 2002, it primarily serves metropolitan Detroit and southeastern Michigan. It frequently receives media coverage for public service.
Tea bag	To tea bag is a slang term for the act of a man placing his scrotum in the mouth of a sexual partner or onto the face or head of another person. The practice resembles dipping a tea bag into a cup of tea when it is done in a repeated in-and-out motion. As a form of non-penetrative sex, it can be done for its own enjoyment or as foreplay.
Social influence	Social influence occurs when one's emotions, opinions, or behaviors are affected by others. Social influence takes many forms and can be seen in conformity, socialization, peer pressure, obedience, leadership, persuasion, sales, and marketing. In 1958, Harvard psychologist, Herbert Kelman identified three broad varieties of social influence.
Psilocybin	Psilocybin is a naturally occurring psychedelic compound produced by over 200 species of mushrooms, collectively known as psilocybin mushrooms. The most potent are members of the genus Psilocybe, such as P. azurescens, P. semilanceata, and P. cyanescens, but psilocybin has also been isolated from about a dozen other genera. As a prodrug, psilocybin is quickly converted by the body to psilocin, which has mind-altering effects similar to those of LSD and mescaline.

11. Caffeine

Substance abuse	Substance abuse, also known as drug abuse, is a patterned use of a substance (drug) in which the user consumes the substance in amounts or with methods neither approved nor supervised by medical professionals. Substance abuse/drug abuse is not limited to mood-altering or psycho-active drugs. If an activity is performed using the objects against the rules and policies of the matter (as in steroids for performance enhancement in sports), it is also called substance abuse.
Stimulation	Stimulation is the action of various agents (stimuli) on nerves, muscles, or a sensory end organ, by which activity is evoked; especially, the nervous impulse produced by various agents on nerves, or a sensory end organ, by which the part connected with the nerve is thrown into a state of activity.

The word is also often used metaphorically. For example, an interesting or fun activity can be described as 'stimulating', regardless of its physical effects on nerves. |
| Mickey Finn | A Mickey Finn is a slang term for a drink laced with a drug (especially chloral hydrate) given to someone without their knowledge in order to incapacitate them. Serving someone a Mickey Finn is most commonly referred to as slipping a mickey, sometimes spelled 'slipping a mickie'.

History of term

The Chicago bartender Michael 'Mickey' Finn

The Mickey Finn is most likely named for the manager and bartender of a Chicago establishment, the Lone Star Saloon and Palm Garden Restaurant, which operated from 1896 to 1903 in the city's South Loop neighborhood on South State Street. |
| Panic attack | Panic attacks are periods of intense fear or apprehension that are of sudden onset and of variable duration of minutes to hours. Panic attacks usually begin abruptly, may reach a peak within 10 minutes,but may continue for much longer if the sufferer had the attack triggered by a situation from which they are not able to escape. In panic attacks that continue unabated, and are triggered by a situation from which the sufferer desires to escape, some sufferers may make frantic efforts to escape, which may be violent if others attempt to contain the sufferer. |
| Risk factor | Risk factor research has proliferated within the discipline of Criminology in recent years, based largely on the early work of Sheldon and Eleanor Glueck in the USA and David Farrington in the UK. The identification of risk factors that are allegedly predictive of offending and reoffending (especially by young people) has heavily influenced the criminal justice policies and practices of a number of first world countries, notably the UK, the USA and Australia. However, the robustness and validity of much 'artefactual' risk factor research has recently come under sustained criticism for:

- Reductionism - e.g. |

over-simplifying complex experiences and circumstances by converting them to simple quantities, limiting investigation of risk factors to psychological and immediate social domains of life, whilst neglecting socio-structural influences;

- Determinism - e.g. characterising young people as passive victims of risk experiences with no ability to construct, negotiate or resist risk;

- Imputation - e.g. assuming that risk factors and definitions of offending are homogenous across countries and cultures, assuming that statistical correlations between risk factors and offending actually represent causal relationships, assuming that risk factors apply to individuals on the basis of aggregated data.

Two UK academics, Stephen Case and Kevin Haines, have been particularly forceful in their critique of risk factor research within a number of academic papers and a comprehensive polemic text entitled 'Understanding Youth Offending: Risk Factor Research, Policy and Practice'.

Alcohol dependence	Alcohol dependence is a psychiatric diagnosis (a substance related disorder DSM-IV) describing an entity in which an individual uses alcohol despite significant areas of dysfunction, evidence of physical dependence, and/or related hardship, and also may cause stress and bipolar disorder.

According to the DSM-IV criteria for alcohol dependence, at least three out of seven of the following criteria must be manifest during a 12 month period:•Tolerance•Withdrawal symptoms or clinically defined Alcohol Withdrawal Syndrome•Use in larger amounts or for longer periods than intended•Persistent desire or unsuccessful efforts to cut down on alcohol use•Time is spent obtaining alcohol or recovering from effects•Social, occupational and recreational pursuits are given up or reduced because of alcohol use•Use is continued despite knowledge of alcohol-related harm (physical or psychological)History and epidemiology

About 12% of American adults have had an alcohol dependence problem at some time in their life. The term 'alcohol dependence' has replaced 'alcoholism' as a term in order that individuals do not internalize the idea of cure and disease, but can approach alcohol as a chemical they may depend upon to cope with outside pressures. |
| Autonomous language | An autonomous language is usually a standard language that has its own established norms, as opposed to a heteronomous variety.

An autonomous language will usually have grammar books, dictionaries and literature written in it. Autonomy is largely a sociopolitical construct rather than a result of specific linguistic differences. |

11. Caffeine

1. _____ occurs when one's emotions, opinions, or behaviors are affected by others. _____ takes many forms and can be seen in conformity, socialization, peer pressure, obedience, leadership, persuasion, sales, and marketing. In 1958, Harvard psychologist, Herbert Kelman identified three broad varieties of _____.

    a. Social influence
    b. Social stratification
    c. Sponsored mobility
    d. Status set

2. A _____ is a social event, often held to raise funds for and/or generate awareness of a social cause or other event.

    The name '_____' is derived from the limited menu which is typically available at the social event: coffee is usually the featured beverage, together with other non-alcoholic beverages such as soda, juice and tea. Desserts and snack foods may round out the menu.

    a. Coffeehouse
    b. Floatopia
    c. Gulf Traffic Exhibition
    d. Jewel Ball

3. In business, _____ is income that a company receives from its normal business activities, usually from the sale of goods and services to customers. In many countries, such as the United Kingdom, _____ is referred to as turnover. Some companies receive _____ from interest, dividends or royalties paid to them by other companies.

    a. Revenue
    b. Salary
    c. Salary inversion
    d. Stipend

4. _____ is a 501(C)3 HIV-AIDS non-profit support group based in Royal Oak, Michigan. Founded in 2002, it primarily serves metropolitan Detroit and southeastern Michigan. It frequently receives media coverage for public service.

    a. Hipster PDA
    b. Higher Ground
    c. Holland Codes
    d. Human Potential Movement

5. . _____s are periods of intense fear or apprehension that are of sudden onset and of variable duration of minutes to hours. _____s usually begin abruptly, may reach a peak within 10 minutes,but may continue for much longer if the sufferer had the attack triggered by a situation from which they are not able to escape. In _____s that continue unabated, and are triggered by a situation from which the sufferer desires to escape, some sufferers may make frantic efforts to escape, which may be violent if others attempt to contain the sufferer.

    a. Perfectionism

b. Panic attack

c. Psychological trauma

d. Psychosomatic medicine

1. a
2. a
3. a
4. b
5. b

You can take the complete Chapter Practice Test

for 11. Caffeine
on all key terms, persons, places, and concepts.

Online 99 Cents

http://www.epub4.1.22005.11.cram101.com/

Use www.Cram101.com for all your study needs

including Cram101's online interactive problem solving labs in

chemistry, statistics, mathematics, and more.

CHAPTER OUTLINE: KEY TERMS, PEOPLE, PLACES, CONCEPTS

_____	Public health
_____	Ronald Reagan
_____	Allowance
_____	Efficacy
_____	Magazine
_____	Enzyte
_____	Incidence
_____	Phenothiazine
_____	Benzedrine
_____	Dexatrim
_____	Mechanism
_____	Amotivational syndrome
_____	Categories
_____	Cocaine
_____	Scientific evidence
_____	Visceral pain
_____	Aristotle
_____	Side Effects
_____	Substance abuse
_____	Survivors guilt
_____	Bronchodilator

12. Dietary Supplements and Over-the-Counter Drugs

	Production
	Mental health
	Identity

Public health

Public health is 'the science and art of preventing disease, prolonging life and promoting health through the organized efforts and informed choices of society, organizations, public and private, communities and individuals' (1920, C.E.A. Winslow). It is concerned with threats to health based on population health analysis. The population in question can be as small as a handful of people or as large as all the inhabitants of several continents (for instance, in the case of a pandemic).

Ronald Reagan

Ronald Wilson Reagan (; February 6, 1911 - June 5, 2004) was the 40th President of the United States, serving from 1981 to 1989. Prior to that, he was the 33rd Governor of California from 1967 to 1975 and a radio, film and television actor.

Born in Tampico, Illinois and raised in Dixon, Reagan was educated at Eureka College, earning a Bachelor of Arts degree in economics and sociology. After his graduation, Reagan moved first to Iowa to work as a radio broadcaster and then in to Los Angeles, California in 1937 where he began a career as an actor, first in films and later television. Some of his most notable films include Knute Rockne, All American, Kings Row, and Bedtime for Bonzo. Reagan served as president of the Screen Actors Guild, and later as a spokesman for General Electric (GE); his start in politics occurred during his work for GE. Originally a member of the Democratic Party, his positions began shifting rightward in the late 1950s, and he switched to the Republican Party in 1962. After delivering a rousing speech in support of Barry Goldwater's presidential candidacy in 1964, he was persuaded to seek the California governorship, winning two years later and again in 1970. He was defeated in his run for the Republican presidential nomination in 1968 as well as 1976, but won both the nomination and election in 1980, defeating incumbent Jimmy Carter.

As president, Reagan implemented sweeping new political and economic initiatives. His supply-side economic policies, dubbed 'Reaganomics', advocated reducing tax rates to spur economic growth, controlling the money supply to reduce inflation, deregulation of the economy, and reducing government spending. In his first term he survived an assassination attempt, took a hard line against labor unions, and ordered an invasion of Grenada.

He was reelected in a landslide in 1984, proclaiming that it was 'Morning in America.' His second term was primarily marked by foreign matters, such as the ending of the Cold War, the 1986 bombing of Libya, and the revelation of the Iran-Contra affair. Publicly describing the Soviet Union as an 'evil empire,' he supported anti-communist movements worldwide and spent his first term forgoing the strategy of détente by ordering a massive military buildup in an arms race with the USSR. Reagan negotiated with Soviet General Secretary Mikhail Gorbachev, culminating in the INF Treaty and the decrease of both countries' nuclear arsenals.

Reagan left office in 1989. In 1994, the former president disclosed that he had been diagnosed with Alzheimer's disease earlier in the year; he died ten years later at the age of 93. He ranks highly in public opinion polls of U.S. Presidents and is credited for generating an ideological renaissance on the American political right. Early life

Ronald Wilson Reagan was born in an apartment on the second floor of a commercial building in Tampico, Illinois on February 6, 1911, to Jack Reagan and Nelle Wilson Reagan. Reagan's father was a salesman and a storyteller, the grandson of Irish Catholic immigrants from County Tipperary while his mother had Scots and English ancestors. Reagan had one sibling, his older brother, Neil (1908-1996), who became an advertising executive. As a boy, Reagan's father nicknamed his son 'Dutch', due to his 'fat little Dutchman'-like appearance, and his 'Dutchboy' haircut; the nickname stuck with him throughout his youth. Reagan's family briefly lived in several towns and cities in Illinois, including Monmouth, Galesburg and Chicago, until 1919, when they returned to Tampico and lived above the H.C. Pitney Variety Store. After his election as president, residing in the upstairs White House private quarters, Reagan would quip that he was 'living above the store again'.

According to Paul Kengor, author of God and Ronald Reagan, Reagan had a particularly strong faith in the goodness of people, which stemmed from the optimistic faith of his mother, Nelle, and the Disciples of Christ faith, which he was baptized into in 1922. For the time, Reagan was unusual in his opposition to racial discrimination, and recalled a time in Dixon when the local inn would not allow black people to stay there.

Allowance	An allowance is an amount of money set aside for a designated purpose.
	Allowing another person to have some money (for whatever reason) is often referred to as an allowance. Types of allowance Allowances in business Construction contracting
	In construction, an allowance is an amount specified and included in the construction contract (or specifications) for a certain item of work (e.g., appliances, lighting, etc).
Efficacy	Efficacy is the capacity to produce an effect. It has different specific meanings in different fields.

12. Dietary Supplements and Over-the-Counter Drugs

Magazine	Magazines, periodicals, glossies, or serials are publications that are printed with ink on paper, and generally published on a regular schedule and containing a variety of content. They are generally financed by advertising, by a purchase price, by pre-paid magazine subscriptions, or all three. At its root the word magazine refers to a collection or storage location.
Enzyte	Enzyte is an herbal nutritional supplement originally manufactured by Berkeley Premium Nutraceuticals (now Vianda, LLC) of Cincinnati, Ohio. The manufacturer has claimed Enzyte promotes 'natural male enhancement', which is suggestive of a euphemism for penile enlargement. However, its effectiveness has been called into doubt and the claims of the manufacturer have been under scrutiny from various state and federal organizations.
Incidence	Incidence is a measure of the risk of developing some new condition within a specified period of time. Although sometimes loosely expressed simply as the number of new cases during some time period, it is better expressed as a proportion or a rate with a denominator. Incidence proportion (also known as cumulative incidence) is the number of new cases within a specified time period divided by the size of the population initially at risk.
Phenothiazine	Phenothiazine is an organic compound that occurs in various antipsychotic and antihistaminic drugs. It has the formula $S(C_6H_4)_2NH$. This yellow tricyclic compound is soluble in acetic acid, benzene, and ether. The compound is related to the thiazine-class of heterocyclic compounds.
Benzedrine	Benzedrine is the trade name of the racemic mixture of amphetamine (dl-amphetamine). It was marketed under this brandname in the USA by Smith, Kline & French in the form of inhalers, starting in 1928. Benzedrine was used to enlarge nasal and bronchial passages and it is closely related to other stimulants produced later, such as dextroamphetamine (d-amphetamine) and methamphetamine. Benzedrine should not be confused with the fundamentally different substance benzphetamine.
Dexatrim	Dexatrim is an over-the-counter (OTC) dietary supplement meant to assist with weight loss. Dexatrim claims it 'gives you the power to lose weight, curb binges, and keep you in control of your diet.' Current Dexatrim products available are in capsule form and include Dexatrim Max Complex 7, Dexatrim Max Daytime Appetite Control, Dexatrim Natural Green Tea, and Dexatrim Natural Extra Energy. The major active ingredients found in current Dexatrim products include caffeine, green tea extract, Asian (Panax) ginseng root extract, and dehydroepiandrosterone (DHEA).
Mechanism	The term Social mechanisms and mechanism-based explanations of social phenomenon originate from the philosophy of science. The core idea behind the mechanism approach has been expressed as follows by Elster (1989: 3-4): 'To explain an event is to give an account of why it happened.

Amotivational syndrome	Amotivational syndrome is a psychological condition associated with diminished inspiration to participate in social situations and activities, with lapses in apathy caused by an external event, situation, substance , relationship , or other cause. While some have claimed that chronic use of cannabis causes amotivational syndrome in some users, empirical studies suggest that there is no such thing as 'amotivational syndrome', per se. From a World Health Organization report: A study done by researchers Barnwell, Earleywine and Wilcox on a sample of undergraduates also suggests that cannabis use does not cause an amotivational syndrome.
Categories	On May 14, 1867, the 27-year-old Charles Sanders Peirce, who eventually founded Pragmatism, presented a paper entitled 'On a New List of Categories' to the American Academy of Arts and Sciences. Among other things, this paper outlined a theory of predication involving three universal categories that Peirce continued to apply in philosophy and elsewhere for the rest of his life. In the categories one will discern, concentrated, the pattern which one finds formed by the three grades of clearness in 'How to Make Our Ideas Clear' (1878 foundational paper for pragmatism), and in numerous other three-way distinctions in his work.
Cocaine	Cocaine is a 1922 British crime film directed by Graham Cutts and starring Hilda Bayley, Flora Le Breton, Ward McAllister and Cyril Raymond. A melodrama - it depicts the distribution of cocaine by gangsters through a series of London nightclubs and the revenge sought by a man after the death of his daughter. Because of its depiction of drug use, it was the most controversial British film of the 1920s.
Scientific evidence	Scientific evidence has no universally accepted definition but generally refers to evidence which serves to either support or counter a scientific theory or hypothesis. Such evidence is generally expected to be empirical and properly documented in accordance with scientific method such as is applicable to the particular field of inquiry. Standards for evidence may vary according to whether the field of inquiry is among the natural sciences or social sciences .
Visceral pain	Visceral Pain is pain that results from the activation of nociceptors of the thoracic, pelvic, or abdominal viscera (organs). Visceral structures are highly sensitive to distension (stretch), ischemia and inflammation, but relatively insensitive to other stimuli that normally evoke pain such as cutting or burning. Visceral pain is diffuse, difficult to localize and often referred to a distant, usually superficial, structure.
Aristotle	Aristotle (384 BC - 322 BC) was a Greek philosopher and polymath, a student of Plato and teacher of Alexander the Great. His writings cover many subjects, including physics, metaphysics, poetry, theater, music, logic, rhetoric, linguistics, politics, government, ethics, biology, and zoology.

12. Dietary Supplements and Over-the-Counter Drugs

Side Effects	Side Effects is a fun romantic comedy about the pharmaceutical industry starring Katherine Heigl as Karly Hert, a pharmaceutical 'detailer', who becomes disillusioned with the lack of ethics in the pharmaceutical industry and has tough choices to make. Also starring Lucian McAfee, Dorian DeMichele, Dave Durbin, Temeceka Harris. The movie's title is a reference to the medical term side effects.
Substance abuse	Substance abuse, also known as drug abuse, is a patterned use of a substance (drug) in which the user consumes the substance in amounts or with methods neither approved nor supervised by medical professionals. Substance abuse/drug abuse is not limited to mood-altering or psycho-active drugs. If an activity is performed using the objects against the rules and policies of the matter (as in steroids for performance enhancement in sports), it is also called substance abuse.
Survivors guilt	Survivor, survivor's, or survivors guilt is a mental condition that occurs when a person perceives themselves to have done wrong by surviving a traumatic event when others did not. It may be found among survivors of combat, natural disasters, epidemics, among the friends and family of those who have committed suicide, and in non-mortal situations such as among those whose colleagues are laid off. The experience and manifestation of survivor's guilt will depend on an individual's psychological profile.
Bronchodilator	A bronchodilator is a substance that dilates the bronchi and bronchioles, decreasing resistance in the respiratory airway and increasing airflow to the lungs. Bronchodilators may be endogenous (originating naturally within the body), or they may be medications administered for the treatment of breathing difficulties. They are most useful in obstructive lung diseases, of which asthma and chronic obstructive pulmonary disease are the most common conditions.
Production	In economics, production is the act of creating output, a good or service which has value and contributes to the utility of individuals. The act may or may not include factors of production other than labor. Any effort directed toward the realization of a desired product or service is a 'productive' effort and the performance of such act is production.
Mental health	Mental health describes either a level of cognitive or emotional well-being or an absence of a mental disorder. From perspectives of the discipline of positive psychology or holism mental health may include an individual's ability to enjoy life and procure a balance between life activities and efforts to achieve psychological resilience. Mental health is an expression of our emotions and signifies a successful adaptation to a range of demands.
Identity	Identity is a term used to describe a person's conception and expression of their individuality or group affiliations (such as national identity and cultural identity). The term is used more specifically in psychology and sociology, and is given a great deal of attention in social psychology. The term is also used with respect to place identity.

1. _____ (384 BC - 322 BC) was a Greek philosopher and polymath, a student of Plato and teacher of Alexander the Great. His writings cover many subjects, including physics, metaphysics, poetry, theater, music, logic, rhetoric, linguistics, politics, government, ethics, biology, and zoology. Together with Plato and Socrates (Plato's teacher), _____ is one of the most important founding figures in Western philosophy.

   a. Ibn al-Saffar
   b. Source criticism
   c. Strong inference
   d. Aristotle

2. _____ is a 1922 British crime film directed by Graham Cutts and starring Hilda Bayley, Flora Le Breton, Ward McAllister and Cyril Raymond. A melodrama - it depicts the distribution of _____ by gangsters through a series of London nightclubs and the revenge sought by a man after the death of his daughter.

   Because of its depiction of drug use, it was the most controversial British film of the 1920s.

   a. Deadlock
   b. Cocaine
   c. The Flying Scot
   d. Gangs of New York

3. A _____ is a substance that dilates the bronchi and bronchioles, decreasing resistance in the respiratory airway and increasing airflow to the lungs. _____s may be endogenous (originating naturally within the body), or they may be medications administered for the treatment of breathing difficulties. They are most useful in obstructive lung diseases, of which asthma and chronic obstructive pulmonary disease are the most common conditions.

   a. Bronchodilator
   b. Canadian Thoracic Society
   c. Certified Case Manager
   d. Certified in Neonatal Pediatric Transport

4. _____ is the capacity to produce an effect. It has different specific meanings in different fields. In medicine, it is the ability of an intervention or drug to reproduce a desired effect in expert hands and under ideal circumstances.

   a. Antonio Commisso
   b. Efficacy
   c. Christopher Ruddy
   d. Sarah Scaife Foundation

5. . An _____ is an amount of money set aside for a designated purpose.

   Allowing another person to have some money (for whatever reason) is often referred to as an _____. Types of _____ _____s in business Construction contracting

In construction, an _____ is an amount specified and included in the construction contract (or specifications) for a certain item of work (e.g., appliances, lighting, etc).

a. Antonio Commisso
b. The Rise and Fall of the Christian Coalition
c. Allowance
d. Sarah Scaife Foundation

1. d

2. b

3. a

4. b

5. c

You can take the complete Chapter Practice Test

for 12. Dietary Supplements and Over-the-Counter Drugs
on all key terms, persons, places, and concepts.

Online 99 Cents

http://www.epub4.1.22005.12.cram101.com/

Use www.Cram101.com for all your study needs

including Cram101's online interactive problem solving labs in

chemistry, statistics, mathematics, and more.

CHAPTER OUTLINE: KEY TERMS, PEOPLE, PLACES, CONCEPTS

	Grief
	Avicenna
	Laudanum
	Samuel Taylor Coleridge
	Confession
	Smuggling
	Dilemma
	Emperor
	Moral
	Codeine
	Heroin
	Perfection
	Patent medicine
	Cocaine
	Drug user
	Hydrocodone
	Oxycodone
	Prescription
	Substance abuse
	Public health
	Chronic pain

13. Opioids

	Nalorphine
	Mickey Finn
	Homeland security
	Mechanism
	Physical dependence
	Psilocybin
	Alcohol dependence
	Inheritance

CHAPTER HIGHLIGHTS & NOTES: KEY TERMS, PEOPLE, PLACES, CONCEPTS

Grief	Grief is a multi-faceted response to loss, particularly to the loss of someone or something to which a bond was formed. Although conventionally focused on the emotional response to loss, it also has physical, cognitive, behavioral, social, and philosophical dimensions. While the terms are often used interchangeably, bereavement refers to the state of loss, and grief is the reaction to loss.
Avicenna	Abu ?Ali al-?usayn ibn ?Abd Allah ibn Sina, commonly known as Ibn Sina or by his Latinized name Avicenna, was a Persian polymath, who wrote almost 450 treatises on a wide range of subjects, of which around 240 have survived. In particular, 150 of his surviving treatises concentrate on philosophy and 40 of them concentrate on medicine.

His most famous works are The Book of Healing, a vast philosophical and scientific encyclopaedia, and The Canon of Medicine, which was a standard medical text at many medieval universities. |
| Laudanum | Laudanum also known as Tincture of Opium, is an alcoholic herbal preparation containing approximately 10% powdered opium by weight (the equivalent of 1% morphine). It is reddish-brown in colour and extremely bitter to the taste. Laudanum contains almost all of the opium alkaloids, including morphine and codeine. |

Samuel Taylor Coleridge	Samuel Taylor Coleridge was an English poet, literary critic and philosopher who, with his friend William Wordsworth, was a founder of the Romantic Movement in England and a member of the Lake Poets. He is probably best known for his poems The Rime of the Ancient Mariner and Kubla Khan, as well as for his major prose work Biographia Literaria. His critical work, especially on Shakespeare, was highly influential, and he helped introduce German idealist philosophy to English-speaking culture.
Confession	In the law of criminal evidence, a confession is a statement by a suspect in crime which is adverse to that person. Some authorities, such as Black's Law Dictionary, define a confession in more narrow terms, e.g. as 'a statement admitting or acknowledging all facts necessary for conviction of a crime,' which would be distinct from a mere admission of certain facts that, if true, would still not, by themselves, satisfy all the elements of the offense. This specific form of testimony, involving oneself, is used as a form of proof in judicial matters, since at least the Inquisition.
Smuggling	Smuggling is the clandestine transportation of goods or persons, such as out of a building, into a prison, or across an international border, in violation of applicable laws or other regulations. There are various motivations to smuggle. These include the participation in illegal trade, such as in the drug trade, in illegal immigration or illegal emigration, tax evasion, providing contraband to a prison inmate, or the theft of the items being smuggled.
Dilemma	A dilemma is a problem offering two possibilities, neither of which is practically acceptable. One in this position has been traditionally described as 'being on the horns of a dilemma', neither horn being comfortable. This is sometimes more colorfully described as 'Finding oneself impaled upon the horns of a dilemma', referring to the sharp points of a bull's horns, equally uncomfortable (and dangerous).
Emperor	An emperor is a (male) monarch, usually the sovereign ruler of an empire or another type of imperial realm. Empress, the female equivalent, may indicate an emperor's wife (empress consort) or a woman who rules in her own right (empress regnant). Emperors are generally recognized to be of a higher honor and rank than kings.
Moral	A moral is a message conveyed or a lesson to be learned from a story or event. The moral may be left to the hearer, reader or viewer to determine for themselves, or may be explicitly encapsulated in a maxim. Finding morals As an example of an explicit maxim, at the end of Aesop's fable of the Tortoise and the Hare, in which the plodding and determined tortoise wins a race against the much-faster yet extremely arrogant hare, the stated moral is 'slow and steady wins the race'.

13. Opioids

Codeine	Codeine or 3-methylmorphine (a natural isomer of methylated morphine, the other being the semi-synthetic 6-methylmorphine) is an opiate used for its analgesic, antitussive, and antidiarrheal properties. Codeine is the second-most predominant alkaloid in opium, at up to 3 percent; it is much more prevalent in the Iranian poppy (Papaver bractreatum), and codeine is extracted from this species in some places although the below-mentioned morphine methylation process is still much more common. It is considered the prototype of the weak to midrange opioids.
Heroin	Heroin (diacetylmorphine or morphine diacetate (INN)), also known as diamorphine (BAN), is an opiate analgesic synthesized by C.R Alder Wright in 1874 by adding two acetyl groups to the molecule morphine, a derivative of the opium poppy. When used in medicine it is typically used to treat severe pain, such as that resulting from a heart attack. It is the 3,6-diacetyl ester of morphine, and functions as a morphine prodrug (meaning that it is metabolically converted to morphine inside the body in order for it to work).
Perfection	In law, perfection relates to the additional steps required to be taken in relation to a security interest in order to make it effective against third parties and/or to retain its effectiveness in the event of default by the grantor of the security interest. Generally speaking, once a security interest is effectively created, it gives certain rights to the holder of the security and imposes duties on the party who grants that security. However, in many legal systems, additional steps --- perfection of the security interest --- are required to enforce the security against third parties such as a liquidator.
Patent medicine	Patent medicine refers to medical compounds of questionable effectiveness sold under a variety of names and labels. The term 'patent medicine' is somewhat of a misnomer because, in most cases, although many of the products were trademarked, they were never patented (most avoided the patent process so as not to reveal products' often hazardous and questionable ingredients). Perhaps the only 'patent medicine' ever to be patented was Castoria.
Cocaine	Cocaine is a 1922 British crime film directed by Graham Cutts and starring Hilda Bayley, Flora Le Breton, Ward McAllister and Cyril Raymond. A melodrama - it depicts the distribution of cocaine by gangsters through a series of London nightclubs and the revenge sought by a man after the death of his daughter. Because of its depiction of drug use, it was the most controversial British film of the 1920s.
Drug user	A drug user is a person who uses drugs either legally or illegally. The term user is typically employed more to refer to illegal drug use by a person who is often part of a subculture of recreational drug use. Drug users are often referred to as 'heads', depending on the drug used, i.e., pothead, hophead, crackhead, etc.
Hydrocodone	Hydrocodone is a semi-synthetic opioid derived from either of two naturally occurring opiates--codeine and thebaine. Hydrocodone is an orally active narcotic analgesic (pain reliever) and antitussive (cough suppressant).

Oxycodone	Oxycodone is an analgesic medication synthesized from poppy-derived thebaine. It was developed in 1916 in Germany, as one of several new semi-synthetic opioids in an attempt to improve on the existing opioids: morphine, diacetylmorphine (heroin), and codeine. Oxycodone oral medications are generally prescribed for the relief of moderate to severe pain. Currently it is formulated as single ingredient products or compounded products. Some common examples of compounding are oxycodone with acetaminophen/paracetamol or non-steroidal anti-inflammatory drugs such as ibuprofen. The formulations are available as generics but are also made under various brand names. OxyContin is Purdue Pharma's brand for time-release oral oxycodone.
Prescription	In law, prescription is the method of sovereignty transfer of a territory through international law analogous to the common law doctrine of adverse possession for private real-estate. Prescription involves the open encroachment by the new sovereign upon the territory in question for a prolonged period of time, acting as the sovereign, without protest or other contest by the original sovereign. This doctrine legalizes de jure the de facto transfer of sovereignty caused in part by the original sovereign's extended negligence and/or neglect of the area in question.
Substance abuse	Substance abuse, also known as drug abuse, is a patterned use of a substance (drug) in which the user consumes the substance in amounts or with methods neither approved nor supervised by medical professionals. Substance abuse/drug abuse is not limited to mood-altering or psycho-active drugs. If an activity is performed using the objects against the rules and policies of the matter (as in steroids for performance enhancement in sports), it is also called substance abuse.
Public health	Public health is 'the science and art of preventing disease, prolonging life and promoting health through the organized efforts and informed choices of society, organizations, public and private, communities and individuals' (1920, C.E.A. Winslow). It is concerned with threats to health based on population health analysis. The population in question can be as small as a handful of people or as large as all the inhabitants of several continents (for instance, in the case of a pandemic).
Chronic pain	Chronic pain is pain that has lasted for a long time. In medicine, the distinction between acute and chronic pain has traditionally been determined by an arbitrary interval of time since onset; the two most commonly used markers being 3 months and 6 months since onset, though some theorists and researchers have placed the transition from acute to chronic pain at 12 months. Others apply acute to pain that lasts less than 30 days, chronic to pain of more than six months duration, and subacute to pain that lasts from one to six months.
Nalorphine	Nalorphine trade names Lethidrone and Nalline. Nalorphine acts at two opioid receptors, at the mu receptor it has antagonistic effects and at the kappa receptors it exerts agonistic characteristics. It is used to reverse opioid overdose and (starting in the 1950s) in a challenge test to determine opioid dependence.

13. Opioids

Mickey Finn	A Mickey Finn is a slang term for a drink laced with a drug (especially chloral hydrate) given to someone without their knowledge in order to incapacitate them. Serving someone a Mickey Finn is most commonly referred to as slipping a mickey, sometimes spelled 'slipping a mickie'. History of term The Chicago bartender Michael 'Mickey' Finn The Mickey Finn is most likely named for the manager and bartender of a Chicago establishment, the Lone Star Saloon and Palm Garden Restaurant, which operated from 1896 to 1903 in the city's South Loop neighborhood on South State Street.
Homeland security	Homeland security is an umbrella term for security efforts to protect states against terrorist activity. Specifically, is a concerted national effort to prevent terrorist attacks within the U.S., reduce America's vulnerability to terrorism, and minimize the damage and recover from attacks that do occur. The term arose following a reorganization of many U.S. government agencies in 2003 to form the United States Department of Homeland Security after the September 11 attacks, and may be used to refer to the actions of that department, the United States Senate Committee on Homeland Security and Governmental Affairs, or the United States House of Representatives Committee on Homeland Security.
Mechanism	The term Social mechanisms and mechanism-based explanations of social phenomenon originate from the philosophy of science. The core idea behind the mechanism approach has been expressed as follows by Elster (1989: 3-4): 'To explain an event is to give an account of why it happened. Usually… this takes the form of citing an earlier event as the cause of the event we want to explain….
Physical dependence	Physical dependence refers to a state resulting from chronic use of a drug that has produced tolerance and where negative physical symptoms of withdrawal result from abrupt discontinuation or dosage reduction. Physical dependence can develop from low-dose therapeutic use of certain medications such as benzodiazepines, opioids, antiepileptics and antidepressants, as well as misuse of recreational drugs such as alcohol, opioids and benzodiazepines. The higher the dose used, the greater the duration of use, and the earlier age use began are predictive of worsened physical dependence and thus more severe withdrawal syndromes.
Psilocybin	Psilocybin is a naturally occurring psychedelic compound produced by over 200 species of mushrooms, collectively known as psilocybin mushrooms. The most potent are members of the genus Psilocybe, such as P. azurescens, P. semilanceata, and P. cyanescens, but psilocybin has also been isolated from about a dozen other genera.

Alcohol dependence	Alcohol dependence is a psychiatric diagnosis (a substance related disorder DSM-IV) describing an entity in which an individual uses alcohol despite significant areas of dysfunction, evidence of physical dependence, and/or related hardship, and also may cause stress and bipolar disorder. According to the DSM-IV criteria for alcohol dependence, at least three out of seven of the following criteria must be manifest during a 12 month period:•Tolerance•Withdrawal symptoms or clinically defined Alcohol Withdrawal Syndrome•Use in larger amounts or for longer periods than intended•Persistent desire or unsuccessful efforts to cut down on alcohol use•Time is spent obtaining alcohol or recovering from effects•Social, occupational and recreational pursuits are given up or reduced because of alcohol use•Use is continued despite knowledge of alcohol-related harm (physical or psychological)History and epidemiology About 12% of American adults have had an alcohol dependence problem at some time in their life. The term 'alcohol dependence' has replaced 'alcoholism' as a term in order that individuals do not internalize the idea of cure and disease, but can approach alcohol as a chemical they may depend upon to cope with outside pressures.
Inheritance	Inheritance is the practice of passing on property, titles, debts, rights and obligations upon the death of an individual. It represents also to pass a characteristic, genetically. It has long played an important role in human societies.

1. A _____ is a person who uses drugs either legally or illegally. The term user is typically employed more to refer to illegal drug use by a person who is often part of a subculture of recreational drug use. _____s are often referred to as 'heads', depending on the drug used, i.e., pothead, hophead, crackhead, etc.

    a. High Intensity Drug Trafficking Area
    b. Malawi Gold
    c. Drug user
    d. Midnight Express

2. . The term Social _____s and _____-based explanations of social phenomenon originate from the philosophy of science.

    The core idea behind the _____ approach has been expressed as follows by Elster (1989: 3-4): 'To explain an event is to give an account of why it happened. Usually... this takes the form of citing an earlier event as the cause of the event we want to explain....

13. Opioids

a. Memetic institutionalism
b. Mentifact
c. Mechanism
d. Middleman minority

3. _____ is a multi-faceted response to loss, particularly to the loss of someone or something to which a bond was formed. Although conventionally focused on the emotional response to loss, it also has physical, cognitive, behavioral, social, and philosophical dimensions. While the terms are often used interchangeably, bereavement refers to the state of loss, and _____ is the reaction to loss.

a. Retaliation
b. Grief
c. withdrawl
d. Carmelo Barbaro

4. Abu ?Ali al-?usayn ibn ?Abd Allah ibn Sina, commonly known as Ibn Sina or by his Latinized name _____, was a Persian polymath, who wrote almost 450 treatises on a wide range of subjects, of which around 240 have survived. In particular, 150 of his surviving treatises concentrate on philosophy and 40 of them concentrate on medicine.

His most famous works are The Book of Healing, a vast philosophical and scientific encyclopaedia, and The Canon of Medicine, which was a standard medical text at many medieval universities.

a. Avicenna
b. Alexander Campbell Fraser
c. Abraham Joshua Heschel
d. Adam Zachary Newton

5. _____ is 'the science and art of preventing disease, prolonging life and promoting health through the organized efforts and informed choices of society, organizations, public and private, communities and individuals' (1920, C.E.A. Winslow). It is concerned with threats to health based on population health analysis. The population in question can be as small as a handful of people or as large as all the inhabitants of several continents (for instance, in the case of a pandemic).

a. Public health
b. Ibn al-Saffar
c. Peter Tudebode
d. Passive-aggressive

ANSWER KEY
13. Opioids

1. c
2. c
3. b
4. a
5. a

You can take the complete Chapter Practice Test

for 13. Opioids
on all key terms, persons, places, and concepts.

Online 99 Cents

http://www.epub4.1.22005.13.cram101.com/

Use www.Cram101.com for all your study needs

including Cram101's online interactive problem solving labs in

chemistry, statistics, mathematics, and more.

CHAPTER OUTLINE: KEY TERMS, PEOPLE, PLACES, CONCEPTS

	Animism
	Rating scale
	Liver
	Psychotherapy
	Cocaine
	Agent
	Criminalization
	Psilocybin
	Chlorpromazine
	Depersonalization
	Hallucinogen persisting perception disorder
	Mickey Finn
	Flashback
	Panic attack
	Screening
	Nora Volkow
	Monitoring
	William James
	Efficacy
	Suicide Tuesday
	Amotivational syndrome

	Derivative
	Reduction
	Bias
	Per capita
	Methamphetamine
	Clinic
	Refusal skills
	Blocking
	Magic
	Indians
	Identity
	Survivors guilt

CHAPTER HIGHLIGHTS & NOTES: KEY TERMS, PEOPLE, PLACES, CONCEPTS

Animism	Animism is the religious worldview that natural physical entities-including animals, plants, and often even inanimate objects or phenomena-possess a spiritual essence. Specifically, animism is used in the anthropology of religion as a term for the religion of indigenous tribal peoples, especially prior to the development and/or infiltration of civilization and organized religion. Although each tribe is unique in its specific mythologies and rituals, the term animism is often used to describe the most common, foundational thread of indigenous tribespeoples' spiritual or 'supernatural' perspectives --- in a word, their worldview, or their 'reality.' Some members of the non-tribal world also consider themselves animists (such as author Daniel Quinn, sculptor Lawson Oyekan, and many Neopagans) and, of course, not all peoples who describe themselves as tribal would describe themselves as animistic.

Rating scale	A rating scale is a set of categories designed to elicit information about a quantitative or a qualitative attribute. In the social sciences, common examples are the Likert scale and 1-10 rating scales in which a person selects the number which is considered to reflect the perceived quality of a product. A rating scale is a method that requires the rater to assign a value, sometimes numeric, to the rated object, as a measure of some rated attribute.
Liver	The liver, hepar, is a vital organ present in vertebrates and some other animals. It has a wide range of functions, including detoxification, protein synthesis, and production of biochemicals necessary for digestion. The liver is necessary for survival; there is currently no way to compensate for the absence of liver function in the long term, although new liver dialysis techniques can be used in the short term.
Psychotherapy	Psychotherapy is a general term referring to therapeutic interaction or treatment contracted between a trained professional and a client, patient, family, couple, or group. The problems addressed are psychological in nature and of no specific kind or degree, but rather depend on the specialty of the practitioner. Psychotherapy aims to increase the individual's sense of his/her own well-being.
Cocaine	Cocaine is a 1922 British crime film directed by Graham Cutts and starring Hilda Bayley, Flora Le Breton, Ward McAllister and Cyril Raymond. A melodrama - it depicts the distribution of cocaine by gangsters through a series of London nightclubs and the revenge sought by a man after the death of his daughter. Because of its depiction of drug use, it was the most controversial British film of the 1920s.
Agent	In economics, an agent is an actor and decision maker in a model. Typically, every agent makes decisions by solving a well or ill defined optimization/choice problem. The term agent can also be seen as equivalent to player in game theory.
Criminalization	Criminalization, in criminology, is 'the process by which behaviors and individuals are transformed into crime and criminals'. Previously legal acts may be transformed into crimes by legislation or judicial decision. However, there is usually a formal presumption in the rules of statutory interpretation against the retrospective application of laws and only the use of express words by the legislature may rebut this presumption.
Psilocybin	Psilocybin is a naturally occurring psychedelic compound produced by over 200 species of mushrooms, collectively known as psilocybin mushrooms. The most potent are members of the genus Psilocybe, such as P. azurescens, P. semilanceata, and P. cyanescens, but psilocybin has also been isolated from about a dozen other genera.

14. Hallucinogens

CHAPTER HIGHLIGHTS & NOTES: KEY TERMS, PEOPLE, PLACES, CONCEPTS

Chlorpromazine	Chlorpromazine is a dopamine antagonist of the typical antipsychotic class of medications possessing additional antiadrenergic, antiserotonergic, anticholinergic and antihistaminergic properties used to treat schizophrenia. First synthesized on December 11, 1950, chlorpromazine was the first drug developed with specific antipsychotic action, and would serve as the prototype for the phenothiazine class of drugs, which later grew to comprise several other agents. The introduction of chlorpromazine into clinical use has been described as the single greatest advance in psychiatric care, dramatically improving the prognosis of patients in psychiatric hospitals worldwide; the availability of antipsychotic drugs curtailed indiscriminate use of electroconvulsive therapy and psychosurgery, and was one of the driving forces behind the deinstitutionalization movement.
Depersonalization	Depersonalization is an anomaly of self-awareness. It consists of a feeling of watching oneself act, while having no control over a situation. Subjects feel they have changed, and the world has become less real, vague, dreamlike, or lacking in significance.
Hallucinogen persisting perception disorder	Hallucinogen persisting perception disorder is a disorder characterized by a continual presence of sensory disturbances, mostly commonly visual, that are reminiscent of those generated by the ingestion of hallucinogenic substances. Previous use of hallucinogens by the person is necessary, but not sufficient, for diagnosis of HPPD. For an individual to be diagnosed with HPPD, the symptoms cannot be due to another medical condition. HPPD is distinct from flashbacks by reason of its relative permanence; while flashbacks are transient, HPPD is persistent.
Mickey Finn	A Mickey Finn is a slang term for a drink laced with a drug (especially chloral hydrate) given to someone without their knowledge in order to incapacitate them. Serving someone a Mickey Finn is most commonly referred to as slipping a mickey, sometimes spelled 'slipping a mickie'. History of term The Chicago bartender Michael 'Mickey' Finn The Mickey Finn is most likely named for the manager and bartender of a Chicago establishment, the Lone Star Saloon and Palm Garden Restaurant, which operated from 1896 to 1903 in the city's South Loop neighborhood on South State Street.
Flashback	Flashback is an interjected scene that takes the narrative back in time from the current point the story has reached. Flashbacks are often used to recount events that happened before the story's primary sequence of events or to fill in crucial backstory. A character origin flashback shows key events early in a character's development.
Panic attack	Panic attacks are periods of intense fear or apprehension that are of sudden onset and of variable duration of minutes to hours.

Visit Cram101.com for full Practice Exams

	Panic attacks usually begin abruptly, may reach a peak within 10 minutes, but may continue for much longer if the sufferer had the attack triggered by a situation from which they are not able to escape. In panic attacks that continue unabated, and are triggered by a situation from which the sufferer desires to escape, some sufferers may make frantic efforts to escape, which may be violent if others attempt to contain the sufferer.
Screening	Screening in economics refers to a strategy of combating adverse selection, one of the potential decision-making complications in cases of asymmetric information. The concept of screening was first developed by Michael Spence (1973), and should be distinguished from signalling, which implies that the informed agent moves first. For purposes of screening, asymmetric information cases assume two economic agents--which we call, for example, Abel and Cain--where Abel knows more about himself than Cain knows about Abel.
Nora Volkow	Nora Volkow is director of the National Institute on Drug Abuse (NIDA). She is the great-granddaughter of Russian revolutionary leader and Head of the Fourth International, Leon Trotsky. Her father was the son of Leon Trotsky's elder daughter.
Monitoring	In medicine, monitoring is the evaluation of a disease or condition over time. It can be performed by continuously measuring certain parameters (for example, by continuously measuring vital signs by a bedside monitor), and/or by repeatedly performing medical tests (such as blood glucose monitoring in people with diabetes mellitus). Transmitting data from a monitor to a distant monitoring station is known as telemetry or biotelemetry.
William James	William James was a pioneering American psychologist and philosopher who was trained as a physician. He was the first educator to offer a psychology course in the U.S. He wrote influential books on the young science of psychology, educational psychology, psychology of religious experience and mysticism, and on the philosophy of pragmatism. He was the brother of novelist Henry James and of diarist Alice James.
Efficacy	Efficacy is the capacity to produce an effect. It has different specific meanings in different fields. In medicine, it is the ability of an intervention or drug to reproduce a desired effect in expert hands and under ideal circumstances.
Suicide Tuesday	Suicide Tuesday is a slang term for the depressive period following the use of MDMA (ecstasy). This term is currently thought to be in use throughout the world where ecstasy is highly used.

14. Hallucinogens

Amotivational syndrome	Amotivational syndrome is a psychological condition associated with diminished inspiration to participate in social situations and activities, with lapses in apathy caused by an external event, situation, substance , relationship , or other cause.
	While some have claimed that chronic use of cannabis causes amotivational syndrome in some users, empirical studies suggest that there is no such thing as 'amotivational syndrome', per se. From a World Health Organization report:
	A study done by researchers Barnwell, Earleywine and Wilcox on a sample of undergraduates also suggests that cannabis use does not cause an amotivational syndrome.
Derivative	In calculus, a branch of mathematics, the derivative is a measure of how a function changes as its input changes. Loosely speaking, a derivative can be thought of as how much one quantity is changing in response to changes in some other quantity; for example, the derivative of the position of a moving object with respect to time is the object's instantaneous velocity.
	The derivative of a function at a chosen input value describes the best linear approximation of the function near that input value.
Reduction	In philosophy, reduction is the process by which one object, property, concept, theory, etc., is shown to be explicable in terms of another, lower level, entity. For example, we say that physical properties such as the boiling point of a substance are reducible to that substance's molecular properties, because statistical mechanics explain why a liquid boils at a certain temperature using only the properties of its constituent atoms. Thus we might also describe reduction as a process analogous to absorption, by which one theory is wholly subsumec under another.
Bias	A statistic is biased if it is calculated in such a way that is systematically different from the population parameter of interest. The following lists some types of, or aspects of, bias which should not be considered mutually exclusive:•Selection bias, where individuals or groups are more likely to take part in a research project than others, resulting in biased samples. This can also be termed Berksonian bias.
Per capita	Per capita is a term adapted from the Latin phrase pro capite meaning 'per (each) head' with pro meaning 'per' or 'for each', and capite (caput ablative) meaning 'head.' Both words together equate to the phrase 'for each head', i.e. per individual or per person. The term is used in a wide variety of social sciences and statistical research contexts, including government statistics, economic indicators, and built environment studies.
	It is commonly and usually used in the field of statistics in place of saying 'for each person' or 'per person'.
Methamphetamine	Methamphetamine is a psychostimulant of the phenethylamine and amphetamine class of drugs.

It increases alertness, concentration, energy, and in high doses, can induce euphoria, enhances self-esteem, and increase libido. Methamphetamine has high potential for abuse and addiction by activating the psychological reward system via triggering a cascading release of dopamine and norepinephrine in the brain.

Clinic	A clinic (or outpatient clinic is primarily devoted to the care of outpatients. Clinics can be privately operated or publicly managed and funded, and typically cover the primary health care needs of populations in local communities, in contrast to larger hospitals which offer specialized treatments and admit inpatients for overnight stays. Some clinics grow to be institutions as large as major hospitals, or become associated with a hospital or medical school, while retaining the name 'clinic'.
Refusal skills	Refusal skills are a set of skills designed to help children avoid participating in high-risk behaviors. Programs designed to discourage crime, drug use, violence, and/or sexual activity frequently include refusal skills in their curricula to help students resist peer pressure while maintaining self-respect. One such program is Drug Abuse Resistance Education.
Blocking	In the statistical theory of the design of experiments, blocking is the arranging of experimental units in groups (blocks) that are similar to one another. For example, an experiment is designed to test a new drug on patients. There are two levels of the treatment, drug, and placebo, administered to male and female patients in a double blind trial.
Magic	Magic (sometimes referred to as stage magic to distinguish it from paranormal or ritual magic) is a performing art that entertains audiences by staging tricks or creating illusions of seemingly impossible or supernatural feats using natural means. These feats are called magic tricks, effects, or illusions. One who performs such illusions is called a magician or an illusionist.
Indians	Indians is a play by Arthur Kopit. At its core is Buffalo Bill Cody and his Wild West Show. The play examines the contradictions of Cody's life and his work with Native Americans.
Identity	Identity is a term used to describe a person's conception and expression of their individuality or group affiliations (such as national identity and cultural identity). The term is used more specifically in psychology and sociology, and is given a great deal of attention in social psychology. The term is also used with respect to place identity.
Survivors guilt	Survivor, survivor's, or survivors guilt is a mental condition that occurs when a person perceives themselves to have done wrong by surviving a traumatic event when others did not.

14. Hallucinogens

It may be found among survivors of combat, natural disasters, epidemics, among the friends and family of those who have committed suicide, and in non-mortal situations such as among those whose colleagues are laid off. The experience and manifestation of survivor's guilt will depend on an individual's psychological profile.

1. _____ was a pioneering American psychologist and philosopher who was trained as a physician. He was the first educator to offer a psychology course in the U.S. He wrote influential books on the young science of psychology, educational psychology, psychology of religious experience and mysticism, and on the philosophy of pragmatism. He was the brother of novelist Henry James and of diarist Alice James.

    a. William James
    b. Mouvement Anti-Utilitariste dans les Sciences Sociales
    c. Rational consensus
    d. Rectification of names

2. In medicine, _____ is the evaluation of a disease or condition over time.

    It can be performed by continuously measuring certain parameters (for example, by continuously measuring vital signs by a bedside monitor), and/or by repeatedly performing medical tests (such as blood glucose _____ in people with diabetes mellitus).

    Transmitting data from a monitor to a distant _____ station is known as telemetry or biotelemetry.

    a. Receptor editing
    b. Refractory period
    c. Monitoring
    d. Visceral pain

3. . In calculus, a branch of mathematics, the _____ is a measure of how a function changes as its input changes. Loosely speaking, a _____ can be thought of as how much one quantity is changing in response to changes in some other quantity; for example, the _____ of the position of a moving object with respect to time is the object's instantaneous velocity.

    The _____ of a function at a chosen input value describes the best linear approximation of the function near that input value.

    a. Differential coefficient
    b. Dini continuity
    c. Derivative
    d. Ditkin set

4. _____ is a general term referring to therapeutic interaction or treatment contracted between a trained professional and a client, patient, family, couple, or group. The problems addressed are psychological in nature and of no specific kind or degree, but rather depend on the specialty of the practitioner.

    _____ aims to increase the individual's sense of his/her own well-being.

    a. Visa overstay
    b. Psychotherapy
    c. Riddle scale
    d. Self-report inventory

5. _____ is a disorder characterized by a continual presence of sensory disturbances, mostly commonly visual, that are reminiscent of those generated by the ingestion of hallucinogenic substances. Previous use of hallucinogens by the person is necessary, but not sufficient, for diagnosis of HPPD. For an individual to be diagnosed with HPPD, the symptoms cannot be due to another medical condition. HPPD is distinct from flashbacks by reason of its relative permanence; while flashbacks are transient, HPPD is persistent.

    a. Hwabyeong
    b. Jumping Frenchmen of Maine
    c. National Mental Health Anti-Stigma Campaign
    d. Hallucinogen persisting perception disorder

1. a
2. c
3. c
4. b
5. d

You can take the complete Chapter Practice Test

for 14. Hallucinogens
on all key terms, persons, places, and concepts.

Online 99 Cents

http://www.epub4.1.22005.14.cram101.com/

Use www.Cram101.com for all your study needs

including Cram101's online interactive problem solving labs in

chemistry, statistics, mathematics, and more.

15. Marijuana

CHAPTER OUTLINE: KEY TERMS, PEOPLE, PLACES, CONCEPTS

Cannabis

Cannabis ruderalis

Nursing home

Absorption

Distribution

Substance abuse

Amotivational syndrome

Coffeehouse

Verbal Behavior

Benzedrine

Codeine

Exposure

Lung

Psilocybin

Controlled substance

Immune system

Survivors guilt

Causation

Decriminalization

Scientific evidence

Cannabis	Cannabis, also known as marijuana, and by other names, is a preparation of the Cannabis plant intended for use as a psychoactive drug and as medicine. Pharmacologically, the principal psychoactive constituent of cannabis is tetrahydrocannabinol (THC); it is one of 400 compounds in the plant, including other cannabinoids, such as cannabidiol (CBD), cannabinol (CBN), and tetrahydrocannabivarin (THCV).

Contemporary uses of cannabis are as a recreational drug, as religious or spiritual rites, or as medicine; the earliest recorded uses date from the 3rd millennium BC. In 2004, the United Nations estimated that global consumption of cannabis indicated that approximately 4.0 percent of the adult world population (162 million people) used cannabis annually, and that approximately 0.6 percent (22.5 million) of people used cannabis daily. |
| Cannabis ruderalis | Cannabis ruderalis is a putative species of Cannabis originating in central Asia. It flowers earlier than C. indica or C. sativa, does not grow as tall, and can withstand much harsher climates than either of them. Cannabis ruderalis is purported to go into budding based strictly on age and not on changes in length of daylight. |
| Nursing home | A nursing home, convalescent home, Skilled Nursing Unit (SNU), care home or rest home provides a type of care of residents: it is a place of residence for people who require constant nursing care and have significant deficiencies with activities of daily living. Residents include the elderly and younger adults with physical or mental disabilities. Residents in a skilled nursing facility may also receive physical, occupational, and other rehabilitative therapies following an accident or illness. |
| Absorption | In economics, absorption is the total demand for all final marketed goods and services by all economic agents resident in an economy, regardless of the origin of the goods and services themselves. As the absorption is equal to the sum of all domestically-produced goods consumed locally and all imports, it is equal to national income $[Y = C + I + G + (X - M)]$ minus the balance of trade $[X - M]$.

The term was coined, and its relation to the balance of trade identified, by Sidney Alexander in 1952. |
| Distribution | Distribution in economics refers to the way total output, income, or wealth is distributed among individuals or among the factors of production (such as labour, land, and capital).. In general theory and the national income and product accounts, each unit of output corresponds to a unit of income. One use of national accounts is for classifying factor incomes and measuring their respective shares, as in National Income. |
| Substance abuse | Substance abuse, also known as drug abuse, is a patterned use of a substance (drug) in which the user consumes the substance in amounts or with methods neither approved nor supervised by medical professionals. Substance abuse/drug abuse is not limited to mood-altering or psycho-active drugs. |

15. Marijuana

Amotivational syndrome	Amotivational syndrome is a psychological condition associated with diminished inspiration to participate in social situations and activities, with lapses in apathy caused by an external event, situation, substance , relationship , or other cause. While some have claimed that chronic use of cannabis causes amotivational syndrome in some users, empirical studies suggest that there is no such thing as 'amotivational syndrome', per se. From a World Health Organization report: A study done by researchers Barnwell, Earleywine and Wilcox on a sample of undergraduates also suggests that cannabis use does not cause an amotivational syndrome.
Coffeehouse	A coffeehouse is a social event, often held to raise funds for and/or generate awareness of a social cause or other event. The name 'coffeehouse' is derived from the limited menu which is typically available at the social event: coffee is usually the featured beverage, together with other non-alcoholic beverages such as soda, juice and tea. Desserts and snack foods may round out the menu.
Verbal Behavior	Verbal Behavior is a 1957 book by psychologist B.F. Skinner that analyzes human behavior, encompassing what is traditionally called language, linguistics, or speech. For Skinner, verbal behavior is simply behavior subject to the same controlling variables as any other operant behavior, although Skinner differentiates between verbal behavior which is mediated by other people, and that which is mediated by the natural world. The book Verbal Behavior is almost entirely theoretical, involving little experimental research in the work itself.
Benzedrine	Benzedrine is the trade name of the racemic mixture of amphetamine (dl-amphetamine). It was marketed under this brandname in the USA by Smith, Kline & French in the form of inhalers, starting in 1928. Benzedrine was used to enlarge nasal and bronchial passages and it is closely related to other stimulants produced later, such as dextroamphetamine (d-amphetamine) and methamphetamine. Benzedrine should not be confused with the fundamentally different substance benzphetamine.
Codeine	Codeine or 3-methylmorphine (a natural isomer of methylated morphine, the other being the semi-synthetic 6-methylmorphine) is an opiate used for its analgesic, antitussive, and antidiarrheal properties. Codeine is the second-most predominant alkaloid in opium, at up to 3 percent; it is much more prevalent in the Iranian poppy (Papaver bractreatum), and codeine is extracted from this species in some places although the below-mentioned morphine methylation process is still much more common. It is considered the prototype of the weak to midrange opioids.
Exposure	Exposure in magic refers to the practice of revealing the secrets of how magic tricks are performed.

	The practice is generally frowned upon as a type of spoiler that ruins the experience of magical performances for audiences. Background
	Exposures are performed by both professional and amateur magicians.
Lung	Lung (Tibetan: rlung) is a word that means wind or breath. It is a key concept in the Vajrayana traditions of Tibetan Buddhism and has a variety of meanings. Lung is a concept that's particularly important to understandings of the subtle body and the Three Vajras (body, speech and mind).
Psilocybin	Psilocybin is a naturally occurring psychedelic compound produced by over 200 species of mushrooms, collectively known as psilocybin mushrooms. The most potent are members of the genus Psilocybe, such as P. azurescens, P. semilanceata, and P. cyanescens, but psilocybin has also been isolated from about a dozen other genera. As a prodrug, psilocybin is quickly converted by the body to psilocin, which has mind-altering effects similar to those of LSD and mescaline.
Controlled substance	A controlled substance is generally a drug or chemical whose manufacture, possession, and use are regulated by a government. This may include illegal drugs and prescription medications (designated Controlled Drug in the United Kingdom).
Immune system	The immune system is a system of biological structures and processes within an organism that protects against disease. To function properly, an immune system must detect a wide variety of agents, from viruses to parasitic worms, and distinguish them from the organism's own healthy tissue.
	Pathogens can rapidly evolve and adapt, and thereby avoid detection and neutralization by the immune system, however, multiple defense mechanisms have also evolved to recognize and neutralize pathogens.
Survivors guilt	Survivor, survivor's, or survivors guilt is a mental condition that occurs when a person perceives themselves to have done wrong by surviving a traumatic event when others did not. It may be found among survivors of combat, natural disasters, epidemics, among the friends and family of those who have committed suicide, and in non-mortal situations such as among those whose colleagues are laid off. The experience and manifestation of survivor's guilt will depend on an individual's psychological profile.
Causation	Causation is the 'causal relationship between conduct and result'. That is to say that causation provides a means of connecting conduct with a resulting effect, typically an injury. In criminal law, it is defined as the actus reus (an action) from which the specific injury or other effect arose and is combined with mens rea (a state of mind) to comprise the elements of guilt.

15. Marijuana

Decriminalization	Decriminalization is the abolition of criminal penalties in relation to certain acts, perhaps retroactively, though perhaps regulated permits or fines might still apply . The reverse process is criminalization. Decriminalization reflects changing social and moral views.
Scientific evidence	Scientific evidence has no universally accepted definition but generally refers to evidence which serves to either support or counter a scientific theory or hypothesis. Such evidence is generally expected to be empirical and properly documented in accordance with scientific method such as is applicable to the particular field of inquiry. Standards for evidence may vary according to whether the field of inquiry is among the natural sciences or social sciences .

1. _____, also known as marijuana, and by other names, is a preparation of the _____ plant intended for use as a psychoactive drug and as medicine. Pharmacologically, the principal psychoactive constituent of _____ is tetrahydrocannabinol (THC); it is one of 400 compounds in the plant, including other cannabinoids, such as cannabidiol (CBD), cannabinol (CBN), and tetrahydrocannabivarin (THCV).

Contemporary uses of _____ are as a recreational drug, as religious or spiritual rites, or as medicine; the earliest recorded uses date from the 3rd millennium BC. In 2004, the United Nations estimated that global consumption of _____ indicated that approximately 4.0 percent of the adult world population (162 million people) used _____ annually, and that approximately 0.6 percent (22.5 million) of people used _____ daily.

a. Marihuana
b. Visa overstay
c. bias
d. Cannabis

2. . _____ in magic refers to the practice of revealing the secrets of how magic tricks are performed.

The practice is generally frowned upon as a type of spoiler that ruins the experience of magical performances for audiences. Background

_____s are performed by both professional and amateur magicians.

a. Illegal number
b. Inevitable disclosure
c. Exposure

15. Marijuana

3. _____ is a putative species of Cannabis originating in central Asia. It flowers earlier than C. indica or C. sativa, does not grow as tall, and can withstand much harsher climates than either of them. _____ is purported to go into budding based strictly on age and not on changes in length of daylight.

    a. withdrawl
    b. Visa overstay
    c. bias
    d. Cannabis ruderalis

4. _____ in economics refers to the way total output, income, or wealth is distributed among individuals or among the factors of production (such as labour, land, and capital).. In general theory and the national income and product accounts, each unit of output corresponds to a unit of income. One use of national accounts is for classifying factor incomes and measuring their respective shares, as in National Income.

    a. The End of Work
    b. Factor income
    c. Distribution
    d. Gender pay gap in Australia

5. A _____, convalescent home, Skilled Nursing Unit (SNU), care home or rest home provides a type of care of residents: it is a place of residence for people who require constant nursing care and have significant deficiencies with activities of daily living. Residents include the elderly and younger adults with physical or mental disabilities. Residents in a skilled nursing facility may also receive physical, occupational, and other rehabilitative therapies following an accident or illness.

    a. Participatory medicine
    b. Patient intelligence
    c. Nursing home
    d. Patient participation

1. d
2. c
3. d
4. c
5. c

You can take the complete Chapter Practice Test

for 15. Marijuana
on all key terms, persons, places, and concepts.

Online 99 Cents

http://www.epub4.1.22005.15.cram101.com/

Use www.Cram101.com for all your study needs

including Cram101's online interactive problem solving labs in

chemistry, statistics, mathematics, and more.

16. Performance-Enhancing Drugs

	Amotivational syndrome
	Amphetamine
	Screening
	Survivors guilt
	Cocaine
	Refusal skills
	Side Effects
	Border guard
	Customs
	Reduction

CHAPTER HIGHLIGHTS & NOTES: KEY TERMS. PEOPLE, PLACES. CONCEPTS

Amotivational syndrome	Amotivational syndrome is a psychological condition associated with diminished inspiration to participate in social situations and activities, with lapses in apathy caused by an external event, situation, substance , relationship , or other cause. While some have claimed that chronic use of cannabis causes amotivational syndrome in some users, empirical studies suggest that there is no such thing as 'amotivational syndrome', per se. From a World Health Organization report: A study done by researchers Barnwell, Earleywine and Wilcox on a sample of undergraduates also suggests that cannabis use does not cause an amotivational syndrome.
Amphetamine	Amphetamine or amfetamine (INN) is a psychostimulant drug of the phenethylamine class which produces increased wakefulness and focus in association with decreased fatigue and appetite.

	Brand names of medications that contain, or metabolize into, amphetamine include Adderall, Dexedrine, Dextrostat, Desoxyn, ProCentra, and Vyvanse, as well as Benzedrine in the past. The drug is also used recreationally and as a performance enhancer.
Screening	Screening in economics refers to a strategy of combating adverse selection, one of the potential decision-making complications in cases of asymmetric information. The concept of screening was first developed by Michael Spence (1973), and should be distinguished from signalling, which implies that the informed agent moves first. For purposes of screening, asymmetric information cases assume two economic agents--which we call, for example, Abel and Cain--where Abel knows more about himself than Cain knows about Abel.
Survivors guilt	Survivor, survivor's, or survivors guilt is a mental condition that occurs when a person perceives themselves to have done wrong by surviving a traumatic event when others did not. It may be found among survivors of combat, natural disasters, epidemics, among the friends and family of those who have committed suicide, and in non-mortal situations such as among those whose colleagues are laid off. The experience and manifestation of survivor's guilt will depend on an individual's psychological profile.
Cocaine	Cocaine is a 1922 British crime film directed by Graham Cutts and starring Hilda Bayley, Flora Le Breton, Ward McAllister and Cyril Raymond. A melodrama - it depicts the distribution of cocaine by gangsters through a series of London nightclubs and the revenge sought by a man after the death of his daughter. Because of its depiction of drug use, it was the most controversial British film of the 1920s.
Refusal skills	Refusal skills are a set of skills designed to help children avoid participating in high-risk behaviors. Programs designed to discourage crime, drug use, violence, and/or sexual activity frequently include refusal skills in their curricula to help students resist peer pressure while maintaining self-respect. One such program is Drug Abuse Resistance Education.
Side Effects	Side Effects is a fun romantic comedy about the pharmaceutical industry starring Katherine Heigl as Karly Hert, a pharmaceutical 'detailer', who becomes disillusioned with the lack of ethics in the pharmaceutical industry and has tough choices to make. Also starring Lucian McAfee, Dorian DeMichele, Dave Durbin, Temeceka Harris. The movie's title is a reference to the medical term side effects.
Border guard	The border guard of a country is a national security agency that performs border control, i.e., enforces the security of the country's national borders.

16. Performance-Enhancing Drugs

During peacetime special border patrolling forces, the Border guard, mans the chain of Border Outposts which are maintained all along international borders by countries to check smuggling, infiltration by spies of untrusted neighboring countries, insurgents bent on smuggling weapons and explosives for terrorist attacks and subversive activities, illegal immigration and human trafficking etc.. Patrols go out regularly from the Border outposts to patrol the international border to check illegal crossings and track any footprints of those who may have crossed over illegally or attempted to.

Customs

Customs is an authority or agency in a country responsible for collecting and safeguarding customs duties and for controlling the flow of goods including animals, transports, personal effects and hazardous items in and out of a country. Depending on local legislation and regulations, the import or export of some goods may be restricted or forbidden, and the customs agency enforces these rules. The customs authority may be different from the immigration authority, which monitors persons who leave or enter the country, checking for appropriate documentation, apprehending people wanted by international arrest warrants, and impeding the entry of others deemed dangerous to the country.

Reduction

In philosophy, reduction is the process by which one object, property, concept, theory, etc., is shown to be explicable in terms of another, lower level, entity. For example, we say that physical properties such as the boiling point of a substance are reducible to that substance's molecular properties, because statistical mechanics explain why a liquid boils at a certain temperature using only the properties of its constituent atoms. Thus we might also describe reduction as a process analogous to absorption, by which one theory is wholly subsumed under another.

1. _____ in economics refers to a strategy of combating adverse selection, one of the potential decision-making complications in cases of asymmetric information. The concept of _____ was first developed by Michael Spence (1973), and should be distinguished from signalling, which implies that the informed agent moves first.

   For purposes of _____, asymmetric information cases assume two economic agents--which we call, for example, Abel and Cain--where Abel knows more about himself than Cain knows about Abel.

   a. Screening
   b. Anxiety disorder
   c. Apathy
   d. Eating disorder

2. _____ is a psychological condition associated with diminished inspiration to participate in social situations and activities, with lapses in apathy caused by an external event, situation, substance , relationship , or other cause.

While some have claimed that chronic use of cannabis causes _____ in some users, empirical studies suggest that there is no such thing as '_____', per se. From a World Health Organization report:

A study done by researchers Barnwell, Earleywine and Wilcox on a sample of undergraduates also suggests that cannabis use does not cause an _____.

a. Antisocial personality disorder
b. Amotivational syndrome
c. Apathy
d. Eating disorder

3. _____ is a 1922 British crime film directed by Graham Cutts and starring Hilda Bayley, Flora Le Breton, Ward McAllister and Cyril Raymond. A melodrama - it depicts the distribution of _____ by gangsters through a series of London nightclubs and the revenge sought by a man after the death of his daughter.

Because of its depiction of drug use, it was the most controversial British film of the 1920s.

a. Deadlock
b. The Embezzler
c. Cocaine
d. Gangs of New York

4. _____ or amfetamine (INN) is a psychostimulant drug of the phenethylamine class which produces increased wakefulness and focus in association with decreased fatigue and appetite.

Brand names of medications that contain, or metabolize into, _____ include Adderall, Dexedrine, Dextrostat, Desoxyn, ProCentra, and Vyvanse, as well as Benzedrine in the past.

The drug is also used recreationally and as a performance enhancer.

a. Amphetamine
b. Anxiety disorder
c. Apathy
d. Eating disorder

5. . _____ is a fun romantic comedy about the pharmaceutical industry starring Katherine Heigl as Karly Hert, a pharmaceutical 'detailer', who becomes disillusioned with the lack of ethics in the pharmaceutical industry and has tough choices to make. Also starring Lucian McAfee, Dorian DeMichele, Dave Durbin, Temeceka Harris. The movie's title is a reference to the medical term _____.

16. Performance-Enhancing Drugs

a. Regulation of therapeutic goods
b. Prescription drug prices in the United States
c. Side Effects
d. Patient Group Directions

1. a
2. b
3. c
4. a
5. c

You can take the complete Chapter Practice Test

for 16. Performance-Enhancing Drugs
on all key terms, persons, places, and concepts.

Online 99 Cents

http://www.epub4.1.22005.16.cram101.com/

Use www.Cram101.com for all your study needs

including Cram101's online interactive problem solving labs in

chemistry, statistics, mathematics, and more.

CHAPTER OUTLINE: KEY TERMS, PEOPLE, PLACES, CONCEPTS

Alcohol dependence

Preventive medicine

National Youth Anti-Drug Media Campaign

Autonomous language

Drug education

Identity

Inoculation

Refusal skills

Social skill

Social influence

Coffeehouse

Substance abuse

Life skills

Initiation

Strengthening Families

Support group

Mental health

Center for Substance Abuse Prevention

17. Preventing Substance Abuse

Alcohol dependence	Alcohol dependence is a psychiatric diagnosis (a substance related disorder DSM-IV) describing an entity in which an individual uses alcohol despite significant areas of dysfunction, evidence of physical dependence, and/or related hardship, and also may cause stress and bipolar disorder. According to the DSM-IV criteria for alcohol dependence, at least three out of seven of the following criteria must be manifest during a 12 month period:•Tolerance•Withdrawal symptoms or clinically defined Alcohol Withdrawal Syndrome•Use in larger amounts or for longer periods than intended•Persistent desire or unsuccessful efforts to cut down on alcohol use•Time is spent obtaining alcohol or recovering from effects•Social, occupational and recreational pursuits are given up or reduced because of alcohol use•Use is continued despite knowledge of alcohol-related harm (physical or psychological)History and epidemiology About 12% of American adults have had an alcohol dependence problem at some time in their life. The term 'alcohol dependence' has replaced 'alcoholism' as a term in order that individuals do not internalize the idea of cure and disease, but can approach alcohol as a chemical they may depend upon to cope with outside pressures.
Preventive medicine	Preventive medicine, consists of measures taken to prevent diseases, (or injuries) rather than curing them or treating their symptoms. This contrasts in method with curative and palliative medicine, and in scope with public health methods (which work at the level of population health rather than individual health). Occupational medicine operates very often within the preventive medicine.
National Youth Anti-Drug Media Campaign	The National Youth Anti-Drug Media Campaign is a current domestic government propaganda campaign in the United States conducted by the Office of National Drug Control Policy (ONDCP) with the goal to 'influence the attitudes of the public and the news media with respect to drug abuse' and of 'reducing and preventing drug abuse among young people in the United States'. History The Office of National Drug Control Policy (ONDCP) was originally established by the National Narcotics Leadership Act of 1988 of the Anti-Drug Abuse Act of 1988, Pub.L. 100-690, 102 Stat. 4181, enacted November 18, 1988, which mandated a national anti-drug propaganda campaign for youth. These activities subsequently funded by the Treasury and General Government Appropriations Act of 1998, Pub.L. 105-61, 111 Stat. 1272, formally creating the National Youth Anti-Drug Media Campaign.
Autonomous language	An autonomous language is usually a standard language that has its own established norms, as opposed to a heteronomous variety. An autonomous language will usually have grammar books, dictionaries and literature written in it.

Drug education	Drug education is the planned provision of information and skills relevant to living in a world where drugs are commonly misused. Planning includes developing strategies for helping children and young people engage with relevant drug-related issues during opportunistic and brief contacts with them as well as during more structured sessions. Drug education enables children and young adults to develop the knowledge, skills and attitudes to appreciate the benefits of a healthy lifestyle, promote responsibility towards the use of drugs and relate these to their own actions and those of others, both now and in their future lives.
Identity	Identity is a term used to describe a person's conception and expression of their individuality or group affiliations (such as national identity and cultural identity). The term is used more specifically in psychology and sociology, and is given a great deal of attention in social psychology. The term is also used with respect to place identity.
Inoculation	Inoculation is the placement of something that will grow or reproduce, and is most commonly used in respect of the introduction of a serum, vaccine, or antigenic substance into the body of a human or animal, especially to produce or boost immunity to a specific disease. It can also be used to refer to the communication of a disease to a living organism by transferring its causative agent into the organism, the implanting of microorganisms or infectious material into a culture medium such as a brewers vat or a petri dish, or the placement of microorganisms or viruses at a site where infection is possible. The verb to inoculate is from Middle English inoculaten, which meant 'to graft a scion' (a scion is a plant part to be grafted onto another plant); which in turn is from Latin inoculare, past participle inoculat-.
Refusal skills	Refusal skills are a set of skills designed to help children avoid participating in high-risk behaviors. Programs designed to discourage crime, drug use, violence, and/or sexual activity frequently include refusal skills in their curricula to help students resist peer pressure while maintaining self-respect. One such program is Drug Abuse Resistance Education.
Social skill	A social skill is any skill facilitating interaction and communication with others. Social rules and relations are created, communicated, and changed in verbal and nonverbal ways. The process of learning such skills is called socialization.
Social influence	Social influence occurs when one's emotions, opinions, or behaviors are affected by others. Social influence takes many forms and can be seen in conformity, socialization, peer pressure, obedience, leadership, persuasion, sales, and marketing. In 1958, Harvard psychologist, Herbert Kelman identified three broad varieties of social influence.
Coffeehouse	A coffeehouse is a social event, often held to raise funds for and/or generate awareness of a social cause or other event.

17. Preventing Substance Abuse

The name 'coffeehouse' is derived from the limited menu which is typically available at the social event: coffee is usually the featured beverage, together with other non-alcoholic beverages such as soda, juice and tea. Desserts and snack foods may round out the menu.

Substance abuse

Substance abuse, also known as drug abuse, is a patterned use of a substance (drug) in which the user consumes the substance in amounts or with methods neither approved nor supervised by medical professionals. Substance abuse/drug abuse is not limited to mood-altering or psycho-active drugs. If an activity is performed using the objects against the rules and policies of the matter (as in steroids for performance enhancement in sports), it is also called substance abuse.

Life skills

{mergefromLife Skills in Canadadate=March 2011}} Life skills are problem solving behaviors used appropriately and responsibly in the management of personal affairs. They are a set of human skills acquired via teaching or direct experience that are used to handle problems and questions commonly encountered in daily human life. The subject varies greatly depending on societal norms and community expectations.

Initiation

Initiation is a rite of passage ceremony marking entrance or acceptance into a group or society. It could also be a formal admission to adulthood in a community or one of its formal components. In an extended sense it can also signify a transformation in which the initiate is 'reborn' into a new role.

Strengthening Families

Strengthening Families is an approach to working with children and families to build 'Protective Factors' that can prevent child abuse and child neglect. The approach is being implemented in early care and education centers, child welfare departments, and other venues across the United States.

Strengthening Families is a project of the Center for the Study of Social Policy.

Support group

In a support group, members provide each other with various types of help, usually nonprofessional and nonmaterial, for a particular shared, usually burdensome, characteristic. The help may take the form of providing and evaluating relevant information, relating personal experiences, listening to and accepting others' experiences, providing sympathetic understanding and establishing social networks. A support group may also work to inform the public or engage in advocacy.

Mental health

Mental health describes either a level of cognitive or emotional well-being or an absence of a mental disorder. From perspectives of the discipline of positive psychology or holism mental health may include an individual's ability to enjoy life and procure a balance between life activities and efforts to achieve psychological resilience. Mental health is an expression of our emotions and signifies a successful adaptation to a range of demands.

17. Preventing Substance Abuse

CHAPTER HIGHLIGHTS & NOTES: KEY TERMS, PEOPLE, PLACES, CONCEPTS

Center for Substance Abuse Prevention	The Center for Substance Abuse Prevention is an agency of the United States government under the Department of Health and Human Services (DHHS) and the Substance Abuse and Mental Health Services Administration (SAMHSA). Established in 1992 from the previous Office of Substance Abuse Prevention, its mission is to reduce the use of illegal substances and the abuse of legal ones. CSAP promotes self-esteem and cultural pride as a way to reduce the attractiveness of drugs, advocates raising taxes as a way to discourage drinking alcohol by young people, develops alcohol and drug curricula, and funds research on alcohol and drug abuse prevention.

CHAPTER QUIZ: KEY TERMS, PEOPLE, PLACES, CONCEPTS

1. _____ describes either a level of cognitive or emotional well-being or an absence of a mental disorder. From perspectives of the discipline of positive psychology or holism _____ may include an individual's ability to enjoy life and procure a balance between life activities and efforts to achieve psychological resilience. _____ is an expression of our emotions and signifies a successful adaptation to a range of demands.

   a. Pardo
   b. Mental health
   c. Primary health care
   d. Richmond Fellowship

2. . _____ is a psychiatric diagnosis (a substance related disorder DSM-IV) describing an entity in which an individual uses alcohol despite significant areas of dysfunction, evidence of physical dependence, and/or related hardship, and also may cause stress and bipolar disorder.

   According to the DSM-IV criteria for _____, at least three out of seven of the following criteria must be manifest during a 12 month period:•Tolerance•Withdrawal symptoms or clinically defined Alcohol Withdrawal Syndrome•Use in larger amounts or for longer periods than intended•Persistent desire or unsuccessful efforts to cut down on alcohol use•Time is spent obtaining alcohol or recovering from effects•Social, occupational and recreational pursuits are given up or reduced because of alcohol use•Use is continued despite knowledge of alcohol-related harm (physical or psychological)History and epidemiology

   About 12% of American adults have had an _____ problem at some time in their life. The term '_____' has replaced 'alcoholism' as a term in order that individuals do not internalize the idea of cure and disease, but can approach alcohol as a chemical they may depend upon to cope with outside pressures.

   a. American Whiskey Trail
   b. Amethyst Initiative
   c. Alcohol dependence

Visit Cram101.com for full Practice Exams

17. Preventing Substance Abuse

3. The _____ is a current domestic government propaganda campaign in the United States conducted by the Office of National Drug Control Policy (ONDCP) with the goal to 'influence the attitudes of the public and the news media with respect to drug abuse' and of 'reducing and preventing drug abuse among young people in the United States'.

   History

   The Office of National Drug Control Policy (ONDCP) was originally established by the National Narcotics Leadership Act of 1988 of the Anti-Drug Abuse Act of 1988, Pub.L. 100-690, 102 Stat. 4181, enacted November 18, 1988, which mandated a national anti-drug propaganda campaign for youth. These activities subsequently funded by the Treasury and General Government Appropriations Act of 1998, Pub.L. 105-61, 111 Stat. 1272, formally creating the _____.

   a. Boliviana negra
   b. Coca eradication
   c. National Youth Anti-Drug Media Campaign
   d. Continuing Criminal Enterprise

4. A _____ is a social event, often held to raise funds for and/or generate awareness of a social cause or other event.

   The name '_____' is derived from the limited menu which is typically available at the social event: coffee is usually the featured beverage, together with other non-alcoholic beverages such as soda, juice and tea. Desserts and snack foods may round out the menu.

   a. Fersommling
   b. Coffeehouse
   c. Gulf Traffic Exhibition
   d. Jewel Ball

5. {mergefrom_____ in Canadadate=March 2011}} _____ are problem solving behaviors used appropriately and responsibly in the management of personal affairs. They are a set of human skills acquired via teaching or direct experience that are used to handle problems and questions commonly encountered in daily human life. The subject varies greatly depending on societal norms and community expectations.

   a. Life skills
   b. cerebral palsy
   c. Down syndrome
   d. Passive-aggressive

1. b

2. c

3. c

4. b

5. a

You can take the complete Chapter Practice Test

for 17. Preventing Substance Abuse
on all key terms, persons, places, and concepts.

Online 99 Cents

http://www.epub4.1.22005.17.cram101.com/

Use www.Cram101.com for all your study needs

including Cram101's online interactive problem solving labs in

chemistry, statistics, mathematics, and more.

CHAPTER OUTLINE: KEY TERMS, PEOPLE, PLACES, CONCEPTS

	Controlled substance
	Buddy system
	Outcome
	Phoenix House
	Motivational Enhancement Therapy
	Self-help group
	Substance-related disorder
	Contingency management
	Defence mechanisms
	Drug user
	Mechanism
	Motivational interviewing
	Mental disorder
	Substance abuse
	Cross-tolerance
	Benzedrine
	Alcohol dependence
	Naltrexone
	Survivors guilt
	Refusal skills
	Anhedonia

18. Treating Substance Use Disorders

	Cocaine
	Cocaine dependence
	Homeland security
	Cannabis
	Mental health
	Compliance

CHAPTER HIGHLIGHTS & NOTES: KEY TERMS, PEOPLE, PLACES, CONCEPTS

Controlled substance	A controlled substance is generally a drug or chemical whose manufacture, possession, and use are regulated by a government. This may include illegal drugs and prescription medications (designated Controlled Drug in the United Kingdom).
Buddy system	The buddy system is a procedure in which two people, the 'buddies', operate together as a single unit so that they are able to monitor and help each other. In adventurous or dangerous activities, where the buddies are often equals, the main benefit of the system is improved safety; each may be able to prevent the other becoming a casualty or rescue the other in a crisis. When this system is used as part of training or the induction of newcomers to an organization, the less experienced buddy learns more quickly from close and frequent contact with the experienced buddy than when operating alone.
Outcome	In game theory, an outcome is a set of moves or strategies taken by the players, or it is their payoffs resulting from the actions or strategies taken by all players. The two are complementary in that, given knowledge of the set of strategies of all players, the final state of the game is known, as are any relevant payoffs. In a game where chance or a random event is involved, the outcome is not known from only the set of strategies, but is only realized when the random event(s) are realized.

Phoenix House	Phoenix House is a nonprofit drug and alcohol rehabilitation organization operating in ten states with 150 programs. Programs serve individuals, families, and communities affected by substance abuse and dependency.
	Phoenix House was founded in 1967 by six heroin addicts who met at a detoxification program in a New York hospital.
Motivational Enhancement Therapy	Motivational Enhancement Therapy is a time-limited four-session adaptation used in Project MATCH, a US-government-funded study of treatment for alcohol problems and the Drinkers' Check -up, which provides normative-based feedback and explores client motivation to change in light of the feedback. It is a development of Motivational Interviewing and Motivational therapy. .
Self-help group	A self-help group (SHG) is a village-based financial intermediary usually composed of 10-20 local women. Most self-help groups are located in India, though SHGs can also be found in other countries, especially in South Asia and Southeast Asia.
	Members make small regular savings contributions over a few months until there is enough capital in the group to begin lending.
Substance-related disorder	A substance-related disorder is an umbrella term used to describe several different conditions (such as intoxication, harmful use/abuse, dependence, withdrawal, and psychoses or amnesia associated with the use of the substance) associated with several different substances (such as alcohol or opiods).
Contingency management	Contingency management is a type of treatment used in the mental health or substance abuse fields. Patients' behaviors are rewarded (or, less often, punished); generally, adherence to or failure to adhere to program rules and regulations or their treatment plan. As an approach to treatment, contingency management emerged from the behavior therapy and applied behavior analysis traditions in mental health.
Defence mechanisms	In Freudian psychoanalytic theory, defence mechanisms are psychological strategies brought into play by the unconscious mind to manipulate, deny, or distort reality (through processes including, but not limited to, Repression, Identification, or Rationalization), and to maintain a socially acceptable self-image or self-schema. Healthy persons normally use different defences throughout life. An ego defense mechanism becomes pathological only when its persistent use leads to maladaptive behaviour such that the physical and/or mental health of the individual is adversely affected.
Drug user	A drug user is a person who uses drugs either legally or illegally. The term user is typically employed more to refer to illegal drug use by a person who is often part of a subculture of recreational drug use.

18. Treating Substance Use Disorders

Mechanism	The term Social mechanisms and mechanism-based explanations of social phenomenon originate from the philosophy of science. The core idea behind the mechanism approach has been expressed as follows by Elster (1989: 3-4): 'To explain an event is to give an account of why it happened. Usually... this takes the form of citing an earlier event as the cause of the event we want to explain....
Motivational interviewing	Motivational interviewing refers to a counseling approach in part developed by clinical psychologists Professor William R Miller, Ph.D. and Professor Stephen Rollnick, Ph.D These fundamental concepts and approaches were later elaborated by Miller and Rollnick (1991) in a more detailed description of clinical procedures. Motivational interviewing is a semi-directive, client-centered counseling style for eliciting behavior change by helping clients to explore and resolve ambivalence.
Mental disorder	A mental disorder or mental illness is a psychological pattern or anomaly, potentially reflected in behavior, that is generally associated with distress or disability, and which is not considered part of normal development of a person's culture. Mental disorders are generally defined by a combination of how a person feels, acts, thinks or perceives. This may be associated with particular regions or functions of the brain or rest of the nervous system, often in a social context.
Substance abuse	Substance abuse, also known as drug abuse, is a patterned use of a substance (drug) in which the user consumes the substance in amounts or with methods neither approved nor supervised by medical professionals. Substance abuse/drug abuse is not limited to mood-altering or psycho-active drugs. If an activity is performed using the objects against the rules and policies of the matter (as in steroids for performance enhancement in sports), it is also called substance abuse.
Cross-tolerance	Cross-tolerance refers to a pharmacological phenomenon, in which a patient being treated with a drug exhibits a physiological resistance to that medication as a result of tolerance to a pharmacologically similar drug. In other words, there is a decrease in response to one drug due to exposure to another drug. It is observed in treatment with antivirals, antibiotics, analgesics and many other medications.
Benzedrine	Benzedrine is the trade name of the racemic mixture of amphetamine (dl-amphetamine). It was marketed under this brandname in the USA by Smith, Kline & French in the form of inhalers, starting in 1928. Benzedrine was used to enlarge nasal and bronchial passages and it is closely related to other stimulants produced later, such as dextroamphetamine (d-amphetamine) and methamphetamine. Benzedrine should not be confused with the fundamentally different substance benzphetamine.
Alcohol dependence	Alcohol dependence is a psychiatric diagnosis (a substance related disorder DSM-IV) describing an entity in which an individual uses alcohol despite significant areas of dysfunction, evidence of physical dependence, and/or related hardship, and also may cause stress and bipolar disorder.

According to the DSM-IV criteria for alcohol dependence, at least three out of seven of the following criteria must be manifest during a 12 month period:•Tolerance•Withdrawal symptoms or clinically defined Alcohol Withdrawal Syndrome•Use in larger amounts or for longer periods than intended•Persistent desire or unsuccessful efforts to cut down on alcohol use•Time is spent obtaining alcohol or recovering from effects•Social, occupational and recreational pursuits are given up or reduced because of alcohol use•Use is continued despite knowledge of alcohol-related harm (physical or psychological)History and epidemiology

About 12% of American adults have had an alcohol dependence problem at some time in their life. The term 'alcohol dependence' has replaced 'alcoholism' as a term in order that individuals do not internalize the idea of cure and disease, but can approach alcohol as a chemical they may depend upon to cope with outside pressures.

Naltrexone	Naltrexone is an opioid receptor antagonist used primarily in the management of alcohol dependence and opioid dependence. It is marketed in generic form as its hydrochloride salt, naltrexone hydrochloride, and marketed under the trade names Revia and Depade. In some countries including the United States, a once-monthly extended-release formulation is marketed under the trade name Vivitrol.
Survivors guilt	Survivor, survivor's, or survivors guilt is a mental condition that occurs when a person perceives themselves to have done wrong by surviving a traumatic event when others did not. It may be found among survivors of combat, natural disasters, epidemics, among the friends and family of those who have committed suicide, and in non-mortal situations such as among those whose colleagues are laid off. The experience and manifestation of survivor's guilt will depend on an individual's psychological profile.
Refusal skills	Refusal skills are a set of skills designed to help children avoid participating in high-risk behaviors. Programs designed to discourage crime, drug use, violence, and/or sexual activity frequently include refusal skills in their curricula to help students resist peer pressure while maintaining self-respect. One such program is Drug Abuse Resistance Education.
Anhedonia	In psychology and psychiatry, anhedonia is an inability to experience pleasurable emotions from normally pleasurable life events such as eating, exercise, social interaction or sexual activities. Anhedonia is seen in the mood disorders, schizoaffective disorder, schizoid personality disorder and other mental disorders. This is considered as one of the negative symptoms of Schizophrenia where patients describe themselves as feeling emotionally empty.
Cocaine	Cocaine is a 1922 British crime film directed by Graham Cutts and starring Hilda Bayley, Flora Le Breton, Ward McAllister and Cyril Raymond.

18. Treating Substance Use Disorders

	A melodrama - it depicts the distribution of cocaine by gangsters through a series of London nightclubs and the revenge sought by a man after the death of his daughter.
	Because of its depiction of drug use, it was the most controversial British film of the 1920s.
Cocaine dependence	Cocaine dependence is a psychological desire to regularly use cocaine. It can result in cardiovascular and brain damage such as constricting blood vessels in the brain, causing strokes and constricting arteries in the heart, causing heart attacks specifically in the central nervous system.
	The use of cocaine can cause mood swings, paranoia, insomnia, psychosis, high blood pressure, tachycardia, panic attacks, cognitive impairments and drastic changes in the personality that can lead to aggressive, compulsive, criminal and/or erratic behaviors.
Homeland security	Homeland security is an umbrella term for security efforts to protect states against terrorist activity. Specifically, is a concerted national effort to prevent terrorist attacks within the U.S., reduce America's vulnerability to terrorism, and minimize the damage and recover from attacks that do occur.
	The term arose following a reorganization of many U.S. government agencies in 2003 to form the United States Department of Homeland Security after the September 11 attacks, and may be used to refer to the actions of that department, the United States Senate Committee on Homeland Security and Governmental Affairs, or the United States House of Representatives Committee on Homeland Security.
Cannabis	Cannabis, also known as marijuana, and by other names, is a preparation of the Cannabis plant intended for use as a psychoactive drug and as medicine. Pharmacologically, the principal psychoactive constituent of cannabis is tetrahydrocannabinol (THC); it is one of 400 compounds in the plant, including other cannabinoids, such as cannabidiol (CBD), cannabinol (CBN), and tetrahydrocannabivarin (THCV).
	Contemporary uses of cannabis are as a recreational drug, as religious or spiritual rites, or as medicine; the earliest recorded uses date from the 3rd millennium BC. In 2004, the United Nations estimated that global consumption of cannabis indicated that approximately 4.0 percent of the adult world population (162 million people) used cannabis annually, and that approximately 0.6 percent (22.5 million) of people used cannabis daily.
Mental health	Mental health describes either a level of cognitive or emotional well-being or an absence of a mental disorder. From perspectives of the discipline of positive psychology or holism mental health may include an individual's ability to enjoy life and procure a balance between life activities and efforts to achieve psychological resilience.

| Compliance | Compliance refers to a response -- specifically, a submission -- made in reaction to a request. The request may be explicit (i.e., foot-in-the-door technique) or implicit (i.e., advertising). The target may or may not recognize that he or she is being urged to act in a particular way. |

CHAPTER QUIZ: KEY TERMS, PEOPLE, PLACES, CONCEPTS

1. _____ is a nonprofit drug and alcohol rehabilitation organization operating in ten states with 150 programs. Programs serve individuals, families, and communities affected by substance abuse and dependency.

   _____ was founded in 1967 by six heroin addicts who met at a detoxification program in a New York hospital.

   a. Phoenix House
   b. Postural Integration
   c. Prenatal and perinatal psychology
   d. Primal Integration

2. A _____ is generally a drug or chemical whose manufacture, possession, and use are regulated by a government. This may include illegal drugs and prescription medications (designated Controlled Drug in the United Kingdom).

   a. Benzodiazepine
   b. Controlled substance
   c. Pharmacotherapy
   d. Pharmaceutical drug

3. A _____ or mental illness is a psychological pattern or anomaly, potentially reflected in behavior, that is generally associated with distress or disability, and which is not considered part of normal development of a person's culture. _____s are generally defined by a combination of how a person feels, acts, thinks or perceives. This may be associated with particular regions or functions of the brain or rest of the nervous system, often in a social context.

   a. Mental health triage
   b. Visa overstay
   c. Mental disorder
   d. Multitheoretical psychotherapy

4. . A _____ (SHG) is a village-based financial intermediary usually composed of 10-20 local women. Most _____s are located in India, though SHGs can also be found in other countries, especially in South Asia and Southeast Asia.

Members make small regular savings contributions over a few months until there is enough capital in the group to begin lending.

a. The SING Campaign
b. Skid row
c. Self-help group
d. Social determinants of health in poverty

5. _____ is a type of treatment used in the mental health or substance abuse fields. Patients' behaviors are rewarded (or, less often, punished); generally, adherence to or failure to adhere to program rules and regulations or their treatment plan. As an approach to treatment, _____ emerged from the behavior therapy and applied behavior analysis traditions in mental health.

a. Contingency management
b. Covert conditioning
c. Cue reactivity
d. Curriculum-based measurement

1. a
2. b
3. c
4. c
5. a

You can take the complete Chapter Practice Test

for 18. Treating Substance Use Disorders
on all key terms, persons, places, and concepts.

Online 99 Cents

http://www.epub4.1.22005.18.cram101.com/

Use www.Cram101.com for all your study needs

including Cram101's online interactive problem solving labs in

chemistry, statistics, mathematics, and more.

Other Cram101 e-Books and Tests

Want More?
Cram101.com...

Cram101.com provides the outlines and highlights of your textbooks, just like this e-StudyGuide, but also gives you the PRACTICE TESTS, and other exclusive study tools for all of your textbooks.

Learn More. *Just click*
http://www.cram101.com/

CPSIA information can be obtained at www.ICGtesting.com
Printed in the USA
LVOW10s2200151014

408996LV00002B/10/P